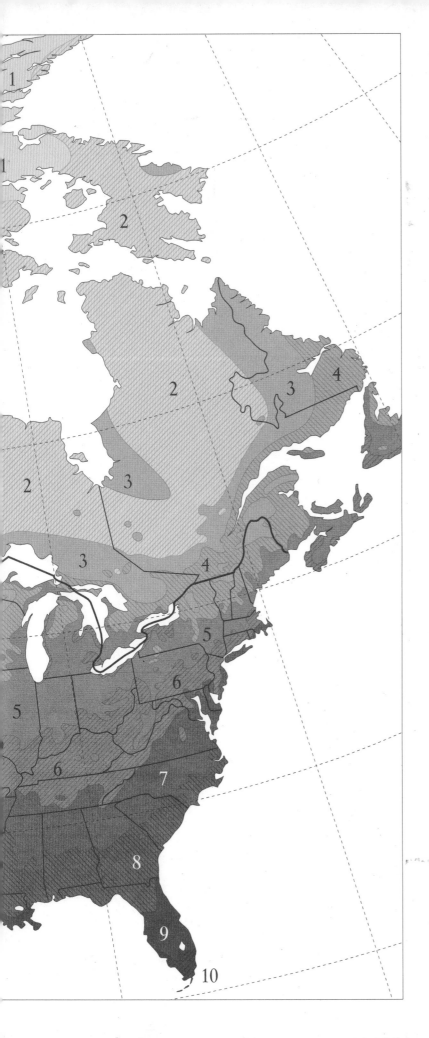

KEY TO HARDINESS ZONES

This ma................es
based o.....................
tempera.................to
1986. The ....ying the
plants in t............cate their lower limits
of winter cold hardiness. Extreme summer
heat and humidity also play a part in a
plant's adaptability; many plants hardy in
colder zones grow poorly in warmer,
wetter ones.

1	**Below −50°F** **Below −46°C**
2	**−50° to −40°F** **−46° to −40°C**
3	**−40° to −30°F** **−40° to −34°C**
4	**−30° to −20°F** **−34° to −29°C**
5	**−20° to −10°F** **−29° to −23°C**
6	**−10° to 0°F** **−23° to −18°C**
7	**0° to 10°F** **−18° to −12°C**
8	**10° to 20°F** **−12° to −7°C**
9	**20° to 30°F** **−7° to −1°C**
10	**30° to 40°F** **−1° to 4°C**
11	**Above 40°F** **Above 4°C**

THE NEW
FLOWER
GARDENER

THE NEW FLOWER GARDENER

PIPPA GREENWOOD

DK PUBLISHING, INC.

A DK PUBLISHING BOOK

To Callum, who was with me every minute that this book was being written and was born just as it was going to press, with lots of love

PROJECT EDITORS
Jennifer Jones & Annabel Morgan

ART EDITOR
Jane Bull

US EDITOR
Ray Rogers

DTP DESIGNER
Matthew Greenfield

MANAGING EDITOR
Louise Abbott

MANAGING ART EDITOR
Lee Griffiths

SPECIAL PHOTOGRAPHY
Dave King

PRODUCTION
Silvia La Greca

PICTURE RESEARCH
Sean Hunter

First American edition, 1998
2 4 6 8 10 9 7 5 3 1

Published in the United States by DK Publishing, Inc.,
95 Madison Avenue, New York, New York 10016
Visit us on the World Wide Web at http://www.dk.com

Library of Congress Cataloging-in-Publication Data
Greenwood, Pippa
    The new flower gardener / by Pippa Greenwood. -- 1st American ed.
    p. cm.
    Includes index
    ISBN 0-7894-3525-X
    1. Flowers. 2. Flower gardening. I. Title.
SB407.G744 1998   98--11894
635.9--DC21   CIP

Reproduction by GRB, Italy
Printed and bound in China by Imago

Contents

INTRODUCTION *6*

Introduction

WHETHER YOU ARE A NEW GARDENER OR AN OLD ONE, NOVICE OR EXPERT, IT IS FLOWERING PLANTS THAT ARE MOST LIKELY TO BRING YOUR GARDEN TO LIFE, NO MATTER WHAT ITS SIZE, EXPOSURE, SOIL TYPE, OR DIFFICULT FEATURES. WHETHER USED AS THE LIVING THREADS in a border tapestry or viewed close-up in a pot or vase, they never fail to lift the spirits. And even though I've lived and worked among flowers all my life, each year their sheer beauty, variety, and complexity of form still take my breath away. It's almost impossible to pick out my favorites – but I have, I hope, made a selection here that even the newest gardener will find easy to grow. I've also picked out varieties that will be easy to find – although a helpful nursery or garden center will always be able to recommend alternatives, if necessary. Whether you have gardened for years or only recently started to try your hand at it, flower gardening is guaranteed to bring you immense pleasure and satisfaction. I hope that this book will inspire and encourage you to get out into the garden and make the very most of your own special patch.

Pippa Greenwood

What is a flower?

FLOWERS LOOK — and smell — the way they do for one compelling reason: to reproduce. To set seed they must be pollinated, and with their flowers they attract insects that will bear pollen from flower to flower and plant to plant. We group plants that will cross-pollinate and reproduce together into species; as in the animal kingdom, breeding between species often produces sterile plants — think of a mule. Within a species, natural genetic variation may act to produce, say, different flower colors, just as families have blue- and brown-eyed children. If a breeder can increase the numbers of an attractive variant, it may be sold as a named variety, also called a cultivar.

STEP INSIDE
Bees rummaging in flowers pick up a dusting of pollen on their furry bodies — they're the perfect vehicle for transporting pollen from flower to flower.

CLEARED FOR LANDING
As clearly marked as runways for airplanes, the dark "guidelines" on the petals of this pansy lead pollinators straight in.

Pollen packed in stamens needs to reach the stigma in the center of (usually) another flower

Flowers open in succession, ensuring that pollination occurs over a long period

Colors in the red-blue range have insect appeal

BEAUTY PARLOR
With its beautiful color and scent, this lily has considerable insect allure — its open shape and prominent stamens ensure each visit is a "hit."

TUNNEL VISION
It's a tight squeeze to reach the nectar at the end of penstemons' funnel-shaped flowers, cozy enough to cover any visiting insect liberally with a generous coating of pollen.

HIDDEN ATTRACTIONS
Flowers like miniature lidded "suitcases" ensure that the pollen and nectar of lupines are well protected from the weather while easily tipping open under the weight of pollinating insects.

Center strongly marked

HITTING THE SPOT
Butterflies love to land, feed, and bask on flat flowers: like the bull's-eye on a target, the center of this anemone guides them in.

FLOWERING LIFESPANS

Plants vary greatly in their longevity and the time it takes for them to produce flowers, and this is crucial to the way we use them in gardens. Annuals rapidly grow from seed, flower, set seed, and die in a single season, while other (perennial) plants, with more of an eye to posterity, flower year after year. These plants develop long-term survival strategies – lying safe and dormant below ground during cold winters, for example, or developing robust, permanent woody frameworks – the plants we call shrubs and trees. Many plants, with even more of a "belt and braces" approach to ensuring their survival, have extra, non-sexual ways of reproducing, so they are not completely reliant on setting seed – their roots and stems spread and form new, miniature plantlets, identical to their parent and capable of independent survival. Gardeners have long exploited this potential, not only to make new plants but also to perpetuate sterile hybrids and to eliminate the possibility of natural variation in named varieties.

PERENNIAL POSTERITY
Perennial plants have the potential to last for many years. Herbaceous perennials such as this *Anemone* × *hybrida* 'Max Vogel' will die back completely in late autumn then send up new growth again in spring. Evergreen perennials retain their leaves all year.

Showy bracts surround tiny flowers

POLLINATING PLOYS
When their flowers are insignificant, as in this euphorbia, plants employ other wiles: scents, for example (not always attractive to us humans!), or, as here, ruffs of showy, leafy bracts that have the same "over here" appeal as petals.

ANNUAL APPEAL
Annuals complete their entire life cycle in one year, so seed is sown, germinates, and produces a plant that flowers, sets seed, and then dies all within one year. Here, a glorious, colorful meadow of annuals, including cornflowers, godetias, California poppies, and daisies provides an easy, low-cost way to produce sensational color quickly.

TWO-YEAR TENURE
Biennials such as these wallflowers need two growing seasons to complete their life cycle. In the first year, biennial seeds grow into leafy plants, followed by flowers in the second year. Most die or are best removed at the end of the second year. Many biennials can be bought as one-year-old plants, which can be useful if you have limited time or facilities.

The flowering year

THE FLOWER GARDEN AT THE height of spring or early summer rarely disappoints – but outside the main season it's often a different story. Yet, with a bit of careful planning, you can create a garden in which flowers are opening almost all year round, generating a wonderful sense of expectation and pride. And when the flowers of the season invite you so appealingly into the garden to care for them, even your least favorite gardening tasks are a pleasure, too.

RITES OF SPRING
Roll out a richly colored carpet for the arrival of spring with a bed of red and yellow tulips, blue forget-me-nots, and rusty red and brown wallflowers. Add a sprinkling of white narcissus and grape hyacinths, and you have something as exotic and beautiful as an intricate Oriental tapestry, with the bonus of fragrance, too.

EARLY START
That time of the year when spring turns into summer can be a tricky period for color in the garden – spring flowers have come and gone, but the full glory of the summer is yet to come. Here, a luminous pink lavatera, *Achillea*, and some early roses step in to fill the gap beautifully. All of these plants will continue to flower for much of the summer.

TOO HOT TO HANDLE
By midsummer, plantings should be lush and voluptuous; as the season reaches its height, let baking borders become a tinderbox of color with fiery dahlias and red-hot pokers, here heightened by the golden yellows and brown tones of the daisylike heleniums in the foreground. This border will still be glowing into autumn.

AUTUMN COLOR

Proof, if ever it was needed, that autumn has its pleasures, too. This superb planting is simplicity itself, with the pink flowers of colchicum growing through (and supported by) the foliage of hardy geraniums as it starts to develop autumnal reddish tints, adding to the beauty of the display.

SMALL WONDERS

Late winter's treasures are mainly small, cool, and very elegant. One of the sights I enjoy most at this time of year is a carpet of *Cyclamen coum* in pink or white dotted with posies of the single snowdrop, *Galanthus nivalis*. With a planting like this, no one could ever suggest that late winter in the garden is boring!

REFLECTED GLORY, *right*

The cloudless blue skies of midsummer are mirrored and amplified to a serene azure in these cornflowers.

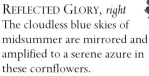

A flower garden calendar

SEASON	SPRING	SUMMER
WHAT'S HAPPENING IN THE GARDEN	With the arrival of spring, the whole flower garden starts to emerge from its long winter sleep. As temperatures rise and the days become both brighter and longer, vibrant new life is suddenly pumped into the beds and borders and everything starts to put on growth: stems shoot up from the dark soil, buds break, and fresh foliage and flowers are produced. In no time at all the gloominess of winter disappears and the garden is studded with the first of the spring flowers.	Summer is a glorious time in the garden, packed to bursting with fast-growing plants covered in flowers. The garden is a hive of activity – both for wildlife and for you. There are lots of jobs to be done at this time, not least a regular patrol of the garden to check for pests and diseases. Toward the end of the summer many flowers are slowing down, producing fewer blooms, so unless it is carefully planned the garden may cease to offer such a breathtaking show.
WHAT'S LOOKING GOOD	Anemones, aubretia, perennial candytuft, doronicums, forget-me-nots, some heathers, lungworts, pasqueflowers, periwinkles, primroses, violas, violets, wallflowers, and lots of wildflowers. There's a host of spring-flowering bulbs to enjoy, including alliums, crocuses, crown imperials, daffodils, grape hyacinths, hyacinths, early irises, snakeshead fritillaries, and tulips.	Acanthus, alchemilla, alyssum, anaphalis, arctotis, campanulas, clematis, columbines, delphiniums, echinops, feverfew, godetia, gypsophila, hebes, helianthemums, hibiscus, irises, larkspur, lavender, lilies, lychnis, meconopsis, mignonette, morning glory, peonies, poppies, sea hollies, stocks, sunflowers, thrift, thyme, verbascums, and most of the bedding plants.
WHAT TO DO	• Early in the season, clear borders of the last of the dead stems and foliage from herbaceous perennials, and remove winter protection in stages as the air and soil warm up. • Plant perennials, especially those plants that bloom in autumn and need a long season to grow. • Get stakes and other plant supports in position for flowers that come into growth early on. • Start to feed plants. Use a high-potassium fertilizer to encourage flowers and a complete fertilizer for boosting overall growth. • Sow seeds – early in spring for annuals and late in the season for perennials. • Plant summer-flowering bulbs such as lilies. • As herbaceous perennials start to reshoot from the base, take basal cuttings from suitable plants. • Divide and replant any perennials that are overcrowded. • Keep a lookout for pests and diseases and control them before they get a hold. • Prune late-flowering clematis early in spring. • Apply a mulch around the base of perennials.	• Continue to feed flowers regularly. Although annuals can be fed until the end of summer, stop feeding perennials after midsummer. • Early in the season plant autumn-flowering bulbs such as colchicums. • Water as necessary, especially during hot weather and on light soils. • Supply stakes and other supports to perennials before they put on too much growth. • Deadhead flowers frequently, but if you want to save your own seed, remember to allow a few seedheads to develop. • Tie in growth of climbers. • Regularly pick cut-flower annuals to ensure a constant supply. • Early in the season, sow more annuals to give color later in the summer. • Make routine checks for pests and diseases, and take appropriate action if any are found. • Late in the summer gather seeds from favorite flowers. • Sow seeds of perennials. • Sow seeds of biennials where they are to flower the following year.

AUTUMN

As the days become shorter and noticeably colder, many plants start to prepare for the winter: growth slows down considerably, especially toward the end of the season. Now is the time to enjoy all the warmth that goldenrod, rudbeckias, sedums, and red-hot pokers can offer. Many flowers that were in bloom earlier in the year now have interesting seedheads, berries, or fruits, and their foliage may take on attractive colors as it starts to die back.

Arctotis, asters, cannas, centaurea, Viticella Group clematis, chrysanthemums, colchicums, crocosmias, autumn crocuses, autumn-flowering cyclamen, dahlias, echinaceas, gaillardia, autumn gentians, goldenrod, hebes, heleniums, Japanese anemones, nerines, phygelius, red-hot pokers, rudbeckias, salvias, sedums, sternbergia.

• Continue to remove faded flowers regularly, again leaving a few *in situ* if you want to allow some seedheads to form to give you seed for sowing.
• Plant perennials – autumn is an especially good season for doing this if your soil is on the dry side.
• Clear most of the faded foliage from perennials, although leaving some in position may help provide protection from winter cold.
• Remove the last of the summer bedding plants and replace them with spring-flowering bedding to bring you fresh color next year.
• Check for the presence of pests and diseases that are capable of surviving over the winter.
• Plant plenty of spring bulbs in borders and in containers, or perhaps even in the lawn.
• Lift gladiolus and dahlia corms and tubers, and store in a dry place.
• Prepare soil for planting later in the autumn or in spring. Dig in some coarse organic matter and apply slow-release fertilizers.
• Lift and divide overcrowded clumps of perennials. Replant the new, smaller pieces immediately.

WINTER

In winter virtually all perennials and bulbs become dormant and die back. Consequently, those that do remain in leaf – or, better still, those that come into flower at this time – are real jewels, focal points in what can otherwise be a somewhat bleak time of year. With careful planning, you can ensure that there is always something of interest to brighten up the winter garden. Site winter plants close to the house so that you can view them through the window regardless of the weather.

Plants in flower include crocuses, cyclamen, winter-flowering heathers, hellebores, irises (notably *Iris reticulata* and *I. unguicularis*), leucojums, early narcissus, snowdrops, and winter aconites. Many plants such as sedums and thistles look stunning when covered in a heavy frost, provided you have left the dead flower stems in place.

• Well before any cold weather really begins to bite, lift all perennials that will not survive winter outdoors and move them to a frost-free spot, or provide winter protection.
• Continue to clear autumn leaves from around plants before they become soggy and encourage rot.
• Plan what you want to achieve and grow next year.
• Order seeds from catalogs as soon as possible while the best selection is still available. Store the seeds in a cool but frost-free, dry place until it is time to sow them.

Giving plants a good start

THERE'S NO BIG SECRET to successful gardening – if you get new plants off to a good start, you will find it much easier to keep them healthy and looking good. The first step is to find a reputable source – whether a garden center, nursery, or mail-order company. This is essential, because you need to be sure that the plants have been properly grown and looked after before you part with your money. Spend a bit of time deciding where to buy your plants and which plants to buy, then you can be confident that you have good-quality specimens. The rest – choosing the right site, planting them carefully, and nurturing them while they establish – is up to you.

BUYING PERENNIALS
Choose vigorous plants with healthy, green top growth – no yellowing leaves, wilting, or signs of pests and diseases. Look carefully and you may find a real bargain – this primrose is ripe for division and will give me three plants for the price of one.

CHOOSING BEDDING PLANTS
Always choose healthy-looking, sturdy plants with plenty of buds rather than flowers – I'll put back the tray of blooming plants, since they have already used up part of their flowering potential.

PLANTING

Planting is easy and should be fun. The steps shown here do not take long, and they should ensure that your plants have the best chance of success. Unless you can guarantee that you will look after your plants well, try to buy them as close to planting time as possible so there is no risk of them drying out or being damaged before you plant them. If your soil is on the dry side, dig in well-rotted organic matter before you start. If it tends to hold water too well, incorporate compost and coarse sand.

1 Dig a planting hole that is wider and deeper than the root ball and loosen the soil around the edges. Sprinkle a complete fertilizer into the soil you have removed, then mix thoroughly.

2 If the soil mix is dry, water thoroughly first. Grip the pot in one hand and support the crown of the plant in the other. Squeeze the pot to loosen the root ball, then invert it to free the plant.

3 Use your fingertips to loosen the root ball, gently teasing some of the outer roots free. This ensures that the roots will soon start to explore the soil around the planting hole.

HOW MANY PLANTS?

When shopping for plants, don't forget that the small specimen in front of you may bear no relation to its ultimate size. If you don't want to end up with an overcrowded border, work out first how many plants you will need when they are *fully grown*, or take a notepad with you, plus the dimensions of the border, and check plant labels for their final height and width. If the border looks sparse at first, fill gaps with bedding plants.

PLANT SPREAD
This young penstemon will eventually spread as far as the outer circle.

PLANTING GROUPS
To work out the spacing between two different types of plant, take the sum of both their spreads and divide by two.

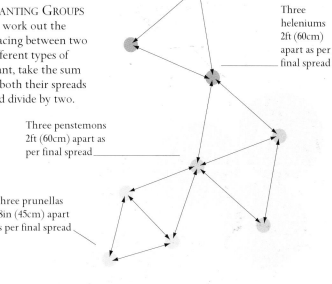

Three heleniums 2ft (60cm) apart as per final spread

Three penstemons 2ft (60cm) apart as per final spread

Three prunellas 18in (45cm) apart as per final spread

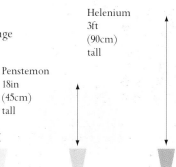

HEIGHT
It's sensible to arrange plants so that the tallest are often at the back.

Helenium 3ft (90cm) tall

Penstemon 18in (45cm) tall

Prunella 6in (15cm) tall

4 Check that the plant is at the correct depth and that the surface of the soil is level with the top of the planting hole. Carefully backfill, firming the soil between the roots and the sides of the hole.

5 Water thoroughly, using a watering can. Fill with more soil if dents appear, making sure that the plant itself is sitting at the same depth as it was when in its container.

6 Mulch the entire root area to deter weeds and to help keep the soil moist. A 2–3in (5–7.5cm) layer works best, spread all around the plant but leaving the area around its stems clear.

Growing from seed

BY RAISING YOUR OWN FLOWERS from seed, you open up a whole new world of possibilities. The range of plants available is tremendous – far greater than that at a garden center – and growing from seed is also fun, especially if you start with some of the easier seeds that don't need extra heat to germinate. The low cost of soil and trays or pots means that this way of stocking your garden is quite inexpensive. Once you have proved to yourself that you can do it, you might want to invest in one of the more elaborate propagation kits and try some trickier seeds.

Some seed can be sown directly outdoors (see pp.20–21), but the range is far greater if you start seeds under cover, as here. If you don't have a greenhouse, place your pots and trays of seedlings on a sunny windowsill on aluminum foil (for added light reflection), and turn them often so that they grow up straight rather than leaning toward the light. Watering the soil mix with a fungicide helps prevent damping-off disease.

SOWING UNDER COVER

1 All you need is a seed tray and some multipurpose soil mix. A new or well-scrubbed tray and bagged, sterile mix reduces the risk of disease. Sieve the mix.

2 Fill the tray to the top. Tamp down the soil mix and level off, by hand or with a small piece of board. The surface should be about ½ in (1cm) below the rim of the tray.

3 Use a watering can fitted with a rose to moisten the soil mix thoroughly. Use clean water, again for good hygiene. If the rose is adjustable, position it so it faces upward.

4 Scatter the seeds evenly and thinly over the soil mix. Try putting the seeds in one cupped hand and gently tapping with the fingers of the other hand to control the flow.

5 Most seeds need a fine covering of soil mix: check the back of the packet. If this is not needed, cover the tray with plastic wrap; this helps keep seeds moist and lets light in.

SOWING FINE SEEDS

Most seeds are fairly easy to handle, but if they are very fine, like lobelia seeds, they are difficult to distribute thinly enough. If you sow seeds too thickly, the resulting seedlings are difficult to separate, and they are also very prone to disease and to becoming etiolated (drawn and yellow). Mixing seeds with sand is an easy way to "dilute" the seeds. You then simply drizzle this mixture onto the soil mix to create a more uniform spread.

1 Mix the seeds well with plenty of horticultural-grade fine sand. Don't be tempted to use cheaper builder's sand, because it may contain impurities that inhibit germination or growth.

2 A piece of heavy paper or thin cardboard with a central fold makes an excellent chute from which to trickle the seed and sand mixture gently and evenly over the surface of the soil mix.

SEEDS AND VERMICULITE

Many fine seeds need light to germinate. Cover them with vermiculite (a lightweight granular material), which helps keep seeds moist and allows some light through.

PRICKING OUT SEEDLINGS

Seedlings need space to grow well, and you will probably need to transfer them ("prick them out") to roomier surroundings as soon as one or two pairs of true leaves have formed (see opposite). Prepare some small pots or another tray. Always water the soil mix thoroughly before removing seedlings from their tray, since this makes the job easier and reduces the risk of root damage.

1 Carefully ease each seedling out of the tray. I use a pencil, but a dibble is fine, too. Take care not to damage the roots, and handle the seedling by its seed leaves.

2 Make regularly spaced holes in the soil mix of the new tray and carefully lower each seedling into its hole. Firm back around its roots, then water or mist.

PLANTING OUT

Most flower seedlings raised under glass will need to be transplanted ("potted up") and grown on again, this time into individual pots. This ensures that each young plant will have a well-developed root system and plenty of top growth before it is acclimatized to conditions outdoors, or "hardened off." To harden off, place plants outdoors in a sheltered spot during the day for several days and bring them in at night. Wait until after the last frosts before planting out.

GROWING SEEDS IN CELLS

Large seeds, or the prepared "pelleted" seeds often available for popular plants, can be sown in individual cells. This method of sowing seeds is particularly useful because it means that they don't need pricking out; when it is time to move them to more spacious surroundings, each seedling has its own well-developed and undisturbed root system.

1 Sieve soil mix over the surface of the cells, then use your hand to distribute it evenly into the cells so that each is filled to just beneath the rim.

2 Insert each seed – here of sunflowers – into a separate cell and cover with soil mix. You can also sow two seeds to a cell, then thin out the weaker ones.

3 Press the base of each cell to release the neat plug of soil mix housing a well-developed root system. Pot on or plant out the seedlings as necessary.

GROWING ANNUALS IN DRIFTS

Not all seed requires an indoor start with trays, pots, and soil mix. Many annuals can be sown directly into the garden, either as "fillers" between perennials or, as here, in blocks to create masses of color. Sowing is generally a spring job, though in some areas they can be sown in autumn. Look at the back of seed packets to see whether the seed is suitable for outdoor sowing and to check timing, planting depth, and spacing.

1 Clear the bed of weeds, debris, and large stones. Dig it over well and make it level. Keeping your feet horizontal, gently tread over the bed to firm the soil and to prevent cracks and settling.

2 Using a rake, gently loosen the top layer of the soil so that the seeds have good conditions in which to germinate. If soil needs feeding, incorporate some fertilizer as you do this.

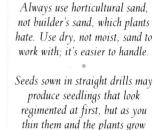

Always use horticultural sand, not builder's sand, which plants hate. Use dry, not moist, sand to work with; it's easier to handle.

Seeds sown in straight drills may produce seedlings that look regimented at first, but as you thin them and the plants grow you won't see the rows.

To stop birds from eating seeds or cats rolling on them (or worse), use netting or stretch taut lengths of twine over the bed until the seeds have germinated.

3 Use horticultural-grade sand to mark out the areas into which you will then sow each type of seed (*left*). Uneven-sized patches will look best unless you want to achieve a more formal look. You may need to use the rake to "fluff up" soil that you have knelt on and flattened.

5 Sow the seeds along the drills. Don't waste seed by sowing too densely, but always sow more than you need; it's best to need to thin seedlings later.

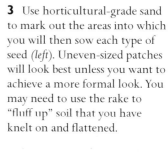

4 Use a stick or bamboo stake to mark out grooves, or "drills," into which you will sow the seed. Sowing in rows makes it easier to tell weed and flower seedlings apart when they come up.

6 Push the ridges over to cover the seeds with soil. Unless rain is forecast in the next few days, gently water the area. As the seedlings develop, thin out where necessary.

Home-grown seeds

GROWING FLOWERS FROM SEEDS that you have gathered yourself from the garden is always satisfying. Some plants, particularly the species and a few named varieties, will "come true" from seed: their offspring will closely resemble the parent plant. Most named varieties, and anything called an "F1 hybrid," produce plants that are not the same as the parents, but the results of these pot-luck plants are often very pretty and well worth growing. Never save seed from plants that are diseased, since some diseases can be transmitted by seed. Always clearly label what you have gathered and when.

Gather seed only when it is fully ripe. If you are worried you might lose it, loosely tie a paper bag around the ripening seedhead.

Gather seeds on a dry day, and not first thing in the morning when they may be moist with dew. Paper bags are best for storage because they won't cause moisture to develop. Store seeds in a cool, dry, frost-free place. If you're not sure when to sow them, take a look at the back of a seed packet.

Gather plenty of seeds, and save only those that look undamaged and healthy. To increase the chances of variation, keep a selection of, say, dark and white seeds, or large and small.

Perennial pea
(*Lathyrus latifolius*)

Hollyhock
(*Alcea*)

RANDOM HARVEST, *above*
For informal plantings where you don't mind what color pops up, some seeds of cottagey plants like these are definitely worth gathering.

IN THE BAG, *above*
Hold an open paper bag beneath the seedhead and tap or shake the stem. Here, the ripe seeds of Jacob's ladder (*Polemonium*) fall readily into the bag.

Case "pings" open to release seeds

HEAD START
Gathering the seeds from *Echinops* (*left*) is easy, but they are then best stored for sowing the following spring. The ripened heads of ornamental alliums (*right*) readily release their seeds when shaken but still leave you with a very pretty seedhead, which you can use in a dried arrangement.

New plants from old

FOR ME, ONE OF GARDENING'S richest rewards is its marvelous sense of continuity – and the fact that you can grow lots of new plants from bits of your old ones has definite economic appeal, too! I still get a real thrill every time I see the first signs that a cutting has taken and is starting to grow on its own roots. Also, while garden centers and nurseries may have a good selection, they can't possibly stock everything, and all too often the particular variety that you have admired in someone else's garden cannot be found. Ask if you can take cuttings or beg a few offsets of bulbs – most gardeners will be only too flattered that you want to imitate their choice.

When taking any plant material to propagate, always select it from your healthiest, most vigorous-looking plants since they should produce the best results.

Experienced gardeners bend the rules when it comes to timing, but you really do get the best results by waiting for the correct season.

SEPARATING OFFSETS

Most bulbs multiply very obligingly, producing offspring, or offsets, around the parent bulb. The clump becomes overcrowded and usually benefits from being lifted and divided. It is best to do this when the plants are dormant, although snowdrops are an exception; divide them after flowering.

In the process you can separate off numerous small bulbs, discarding any that look unhealthy, and replant them immediately on freshly prepared ground. They may take a year or more to reach flowering size, so keep them in a less prominent area and feed well until they are large enough to flower.

Parent bulb

Young offsets

Put a label in the ground by your newly planted offsets so that you know what you have planted, and where.

Avoid using offsets from bulbs with foliage that show signs of disease, such as streaking.

CUTTINGS

Softwood cuttings are young, succulent shoots, either the tips of new stems, cut about six leaves down (usually in late spring or early summer), or early shoots that spring from the crown of the plant (basal cuttings). Semiripe cuttings are taken when growth is starting to turn woody, usually in mid- to late summer, again cutting about six leaves down, except in some shrubbier plants, where you pull off a sideshoot with a tag, or heel, of bark from the main stem.

TAKING CUTTINGS WITH A HEEL

1 If the cutting requires a heel, carefully pull the shoot you want away from the main stem so that it comes away with the swelling at the joint attached to the base.

2 Always choose healthy, vigorous-looking stems for cuttings. Once the cutting is separated from the plant you can clearly see the heel with a small strip of bark attached.

3 Hold the cutting firmly and use a sharp knife carefully to cut off any excess bark, neatening up the edge of the heel in the process. Plant as soon as possible and do not leave in bright sunlight.

DIVIDING FLESHY ROOTS

Some plants – such as irises and bergenias – have thick, fleshy structures, called rhizomes, close to the soil surface. As the plant forms a spreading clump, the rhizomes in the middle become old and bare. Division allows you to rejuvenate the clump and gain extra plants. Drive a fork in at an angle well away from the clump to minimize injury, lift the rhizomes, and shake off excess soil.

1 Separate the rhizomes, discard any that look unhealthy, and keep those parts that are vigorous. Dusting cut surfaces with sulfur helps keep them disease free.

2 Use a sharp knife or scissors to cut back the foliage. This helps keep the new plant stable in the ground and reduces moisture loss from the foliage.

3 Each rhizome section looks healthy and has sufficient roots attached to keep it alive until more form. Plant the rhizomes close to the soil surface.

DIVIDING CLUMPS

Most clump-forming herbaceous perennials, especially those that have a wide-spreading root system or lots of basal shoots, are easy to divide, giving you several new, small but reinvigorated plants. This is best done in autumn or early spring. When you lift the plant, take the opportunity to weed the surrounding soil thoroughly, and fork in some organic matter.

1 After lifting, pull or cut the plant into sections. Divide large or tough clumps by inserting two forks back to back into the clump to pry it apart.

2 Separate each division using a sharp knife, then neaten cut surfaces. Replant the sections immediately, choosing the healthiest and most vigorous.

Make sure that each section has plenty of thin, fibrous feeding roots. Divide plants in a cool, shady spot to keep them in good condition. Once replanted, keep well watered and protected from temperature extremes.

Divide autumn-flowering plants in spring and spring-blooming plants in autumn.

ROOTING CUTTINGS

1 Remove the lowest leaves to leave about 2in (5cm) of clear stem. Dip the base of the cutting in hormone rooting powder (to stimulate root formation) and tap sharply to shake off excess.

2 Insert the cutting into the soil mix and firm the mix carefully against its base. Water well with clean water. Keep well watered and provide bottom heat if necessary.

STARTING CUTTINGS OFF
Use a small pot to encourage the roots to grow out to the sides.

Take cuttings early in the day when the plants show no signs of heat stress.

Check the requirements of your cuttings — some do better in humid conditions; some may need the heat of a propagating case. The type of soil mix they will thrive in also varies.

Water cuttings with clean water, and keep a fungicide on hand just in case.

Keeping up appearances

ONE OF THE MOST USEFUL JOBS you can do in the garden is to walk around inspecting it regularly. By nipping out a dead flowerhead or new weed here, or making a mental note of overcrowding or some slug damage there, you can keep the garden looking great and stop little jobs from piling up to become a weekend slog. Allow plenty of time to admire your handiwork, and it'll hardly seem like work at all!

WATERING

An adequate and regular supply of water is essential for most flowers. Water needs will vary depending on the plant, the site, the season, and weather conditions, but there are several general rules that are worth observing. Always water gently, taking care to avoid eroding the soil from around the base of the plant. This gives water time to seep down to the roots, reducing runoff. It's best to water in the early evening, especially in hot weather, minimizing loss due to evaporation.

To conserve water, set the plant in a slight depression or insert a pipe to run from the soil surface down to the root ball.

Add water-retaining polymer granules to containers; check the package for the correct amount.

If the soil is very dry, to reduce runoff, water it briefly to moisten the surface, then water thoroughly shortly afterward.

FEEDING

Although many garden soils contain a good range of plant nutrients, it is worth adding some fertilizer to ensure that plants receive plenty of everything they need to flower well. There are many different types, organic and inorganic, which come in the form of liquids, powders, granules, controlled-release pellets, or sticks. Some contain a broad spectrum of nutrients and may be described as "general," or"complete"; others are more restricted in content and serve a specific purpose.

Wear gloves when handling granular fertilizers, and avoid sprinkling them on the plant.

Always check the product label for the N:P:K ratio — the ratio of nitrogen to phosphorus to potassium — and other information as to what the fertilizer is best used for.

Check timing and quantities before you apply; fertilizer applied in the wrong season or amount may be of little benefit.

MULCHING

A layer of mulch added to the soil surface helps reduce moisture loss from the soil due to evaporation and helps deter weeds. I prefer to use natural material that allows water to reach the roots such as composted bark, bark chips, cocoa shells, or gravel, although black plastic is also an option. Before mulching, remove weeds and water the soil thoroughly first. Mulch the whole bed or at least each individual plant's root area, leaving a small circle clear around the crown.

Gravel is an effective mulch that can be laid directly on the surface of the soil or used to camouflage a layer of black plastic. It will require little or no maintenance.

DEADHEADING

Removing faded flowerheads makes a difference to a plant's performance. Unless those shriveled, unattractive brown flowers are removed promptly, the plant usually starts to produce a seedhead, fruit, or pod. This means that both the number of flowers produced and the length of the flowering period start to decrease. There is also a risk that fungi such as gray mold will invade the dead flower and possibly kill the plant. To be most effective, deadhead regularly and as soon as the flowers have faded.

SHORT-STEMMED FLOWERS
Plants that produce lots of flowers in quick succession like these petunias need very frequent deadheading. Since each individual flower stem is short, just pinch off the faded blooms.

PROVIDING SUPPORT

Supports help keep plants compact when they might otherwise tend to flop and ensure that unwieldy flower stems remain straight and unbroken. Always get stakes or other plant supports in position as early as possible so that the plant develops naturally around them.

READY-MADE SUPPORT
Specifically made, plastic-coated or galvanized wire supports have individual sections that link together to create a support of the precise size and shape you need. Ideal for floppy leaves, they are soon hidden as plants grow.

SINGLE STAKE
Tall, heavy, individual flower stems – here of a delphinium – often need support. Insert a stake close to the crown and tie the flower stem to it at intervals as it develops. To prevent eye injury, top with a stake guard.

TWIGGY STICKS
A subtle support system is easy to construct using twiggy sticks driven into the soil around the crown of the plant. Use them for plants with delicate stems or for patio container plants for an elegant effect.

STAKES AND TWINE
Vigorously growing plants may need sturdier support to prevent flopping, especially in windy sites. Drive several stakes into the soil around the main mass of the plant, then tie garden twine so that it links the stakes together.

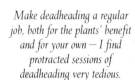

LONG-STEMMED FLOWERS
For most plants that have long, bare flower stems, such as this rudbeckia, it is best to cut the entire flower stem, complete with the faded bloom, down to its point of origin at a main stem.

FLOWERHEADS AND SPIKES
Use pruners or sharp scissors to remove just the faded flowerheads from flower stems that carry leaves, which are useful to the plant; there may also be more flower buds lower down.

TRIMMING
With some plants such as lavender you can deadhead all at once and neaten the plant, too, by giving it a quick "haircut" with shears. This also helps encourage dense, bushy growth.

Make deadheading a regular job, both for the plants' benefit and for your own – I find protracted sessions of deadheading very tedious.

If you want to save some seed, remove all but a few developing seedheads, and you should still get plenty of flowers.

Periods of heavy summer rain often damage petals, so you may find there is plenty of deadheading to do afterward.

Secrets of success

HOWEVER CAREFULLY YOU CHOOSE your plants and then nurture them, both pests and diseases and extremes of weather are likely to cause problems at some stage. Although such problems may be disheartening, they are rarely very serious, and the plant can usually be restored to good health without your needing to expend a great deal of effort. If there's no option but to lose a plant, don't be despondent – as the wisest gardeners say, a dead plant isn't a failure but a wonderful new planting opportunity!

Make a note of when you carry out seasonal tasks so that you will remember to do them at the correct time in the future. For example, if late frosts occur, mark the date in your garden diary so you don't remove winter protection too early.

YOUR FRIENDS IN THE GARDEN

Not all wildlife visitors to your garden are pests. Many of them are very beneficial, and, provided you can supply them with at least some of their habitat needs, they will reward you with cost-free, natural pest control. Any water feature – especially a pond – acts like a magnet, enticing many potentially useful animals, which use the water for drinking, grooming, or breeding. Growing a wide range of plants helps, too, particularly if you can include some that have plenty of readily accessible nectar (see Flowers for Bees and Butterflies, pp.138–139). Being too neat and clearing up all debris and dead plant material at the end of the season may discourage garden friends. You may be removing their breeding or overwintering places, so always try to leave a few hideaways.

Ladybug feeding on aphids

Use pesticides only when absolutely necessary. Choose products that specifically target the problem, minimizing damage to other creatures.

Plenty of insects are either harmless or beneficial. Relatively few are pests, so always identify them before you spray or squash!

DISEASE AND PEST PATROL

Keeping your eyes open as you go around the garden is often all it takes to keep many pests and diseases in check. Take a container with you and gather and dispose of the culprits or the affected leaves. By taking such simple measures it may be possible to stop potentially serious problems in their tracks. If you don't want to use chemicals at all, you may just need to dispose of badly infested plants. After a few seasons you will get to know the "high-risk" plants in your garden and perhaps consider alternatives.

POWDERY MILDEW
If this grayish white fungal layer appears (often in dry spells), pick off affected leaves or other plant parts. Keep plants well watered at the roots, but avoid wetting the foliage. Consider spraying with a suitable fungicide.

GRAY MOLD (BOTRYTIS)
Avoid injuring plants and remove dead or damaged areas promptly, before they're attacked by this fuzzy gray fungal growth. Poor air circulation encourages it, so separate crowded plants. Consider spraying with a fungicide.

APHIDS
Aphids of many kinds feed by sucking plant sap, often causing distortion and poor growth, and may spread viruses, too. Spray with a suitable insecticide, preferably one containing a contact insecticide.

EXTREMES OF TEMPERATURE

Plants may need protecting against weather extremes, especially when they are newly planted and not yet properly established. In cold climates, protection may enable you to keep plants over winter that otherwise would not survive. The protection need not be expensive or too time-consuming to provide, and the benefits are usually well worth any effort involved.

Never buy and plant out summer bedding too early, however tempting it may look in the garden center.

Plants sold as summer bedding aren't meant to live through winter. Even if a few scruffy specimens miraculously survive, they're better replaced with strong young plants.

SUMMER PROTECTION
Some plants, particularly clematis, may enjoy a sunny fence or wall over which to scramble, but at the same time need to have their roots kept cool if they are to thrive. Placing old roof tiles, slates, or pebbles around the base solves the problem, keeping the soil shaded and retaining moisture. They have the added bonus that they can be arranged to look decorative, too.

WINTER PROTECTION
Plants in containers are particularly prone to cold damage because they are grown above ground. Soil moisture may also be unavailable. Wrapping the whole container securely in burlap affords the plant protection. Old curtains, bubblewrap, black plastic, or similar material will work just as efficiently, although as far as appearance goes the effect will be less attractive.

MULCHING FOR SURVIVAL
Covering marginally hardy perennials with a deep, loose mulch may often be sufficient to allow them to survive a "normal" winter. It may mean you do not need to lift the plants each autumn and is especially useful for plants that are young or recently planted, which are often more susceptible. Use materials such as loose straw or leaves, since winter moisture is often just as damaging as low temperatures.

CATERPILLARS
Most caterpillars feed in groups on leaves, leaving holes. They usually feed after dusk, so check plants at this time. Pick off by hand if possible, or spray affected plants with a suitable insecticide or biological control.

EARWIGS
Often feeding at night and eating extensive holes in flower buds, petals, and young leaves, these pests often hide among the plants during the day. Set earwig traps or consider spraying with a suitable insecticide.

SLUGS AND SNAILS
These cause extensive damage to flowers, foliage, and stems, especially soft young growth. Damp evenings are their favorite dining time. Set traps, create barriers, or consider using biological controls.

Brand names and formulations of garden chemicals do often change, but good garden centers will always have someone available who can recommend a suitable preparation for your plant problem. And if the term "biological control" is new to you, ask about this, too: these tiny organisms, bought in package form, will go to war against many pests on your behalf. Though they are more expensive, they are an environmentally friendly way of banishing pests.

Spikes & spires

HOW FLAT THE FLOWER GARDEN WOULD BE WITHOUT SPIKES AND SPIRES. FROM THE COOL, SECRETIVE BEAUTY OF FOXGLOVES TO MASSED RANKS OF COLORFUL SALVIAS, THESE PLANTS HAVE UNDENIABLE poise and impact. But, despite their stature and presence, few of them could be accused of being standoffish – many owe their popularity to the cottage gardeners of old, and they are just as happy in a more relaxed, rustic planting as in a formal border. On most, the flowers open gradually over a long period, and this, combined with their striking, often pencil-thin outlines and a tremendous range of colors and heights, makes spikes and spires invaluable in any garden, large or small. Most make ideal candidates for the back or middle of a border, but a clump of tall spires on its own also makes a fantastic focal point.

"Who can resist these elegant yet sturdy spires as they stand like straight-backed soldiers on parade?"

DELPHINIUMS, PAGES 32–33

LEFT FOXGLOVES (PP.42–43), COOL AND ELEGANT IN A WOODLAND SETTING

Delphiniums *Delphinium*

WHO CAN RESIST THESE elegant yet sturdy spires as they stand like straight-backed soldiers on parade? Despite this air of formality, delphiniums are surprisingly versatile, and they are as much at home in a cottage-style garden as in a traditional, elaborate herbaceous border. Even when they are not in flower, their lush foliage forms an attractive mound, provided you can keep it free from the ravages of slugs!

◄ FLOWER
SPIKE
10in (25cm)
long

CREAM ON TOP, *above*
'Sungleam' has creamy white
flower spikes with yellow centers,
mixing well with other colors.

WHITER THAN WHITE, *left*
The flowers of 'Clear Spring'
are tightly packed together
along its stems, creating
impressive, pure white
towers in summer.

BROWN-EYED GIRL
The semidouble, delicate pink,
brown-eyed flower spikes of
'Rosemary Brock' look lovely
planted with the lilac-mauve
delphinium 'Conspicuous'.

ROYAL FLUSH
The small, delicate flowers of
'Atlantis', a Belladonna Group
member, are a truly regal purple
and their fine foliage matches
their elegant demeanor.

GROWING DELPHINIUMS

CROWNING GLORY

The towering spikes of tall delphiniums are ideal for the back of the flower border; plant them in groups for maximum impact. Place medium to small varieties closer to the front, where they will add stature without obscuring the view to plants behind.

Where possible, plant delphiniums out of prevailing winds. Support flower spikes with sturdy stakes early in the season and with care, avoiding injury to the base of the plant. Twiggy branches are fine for dwarf varieties.

PLANT PROFILE

Perennials, though the Pacific Hybrids – 'Black Knight', 'King Arthur', and so on – are usually short-lived. Z 3–7.

- SIZE 3–6ft (90–180cm).
- FLOWER COLORS Red, blue, purple, lilac, pink, white.
- FLOWERING Early to mid-summer.
- SITE Best in reasonably well-drained, rich soil, in full sun, in areas with cool summers.

Sowing Seed can be sown directly into the soil in spring. The seeds do not last long and are best sown as soon as possible after collection or after the packet has been opened. To keep seed over winter, store at 36–41°F (2–5°C) until you can sow them.

Dividing Divide established plants in spring, or take basal cuttings in spring.

Flower care As soon as the flower spike has faded, cut back to a vigorous, healthy leaf. This not only cleans up the plant but often encourages a second, later flush of flowers.

For cutting Delphiniums make excellent cut flowers. Cut just as the first buds start to open.

My favorites 'Blue Bird'; 'Blue Dawn'; 'Blue Fountains'; 'Blue Nile'; 'Bruce'; 'Butterball'; *Delphinium cardinale*; 'Centurion Sky Blue'; 'Chelsea Star'; 'Dwarf Snow White'; *D. grandiflorum, D. g.* 'Blue Butterfly'; 'Strawberry Fair'; and the Pacific Hybrids 'Astolat', 'Black Knight', 'Cameliard', 'Galahad', 'Guinevere', 'King Arthur'.

BLUE CLASSIC, *right*

For a really traditional delphinium, this fantastic form of 'Clear Spring' is hard to beat. Its purple-blue flowers each have a contrasting ruffled white center and are closely packed on sturdy stems.

◄ FLOWER SPIKE
16in (40cm) long

Penstemons *PENSTEMON*

FORMING CLUMPS OF TALL, graceful flower stems year after year, penstemons are excellent value. They are easy to look after, they don't need staking or pruning, and they will flower throughout the summer and into mid-autumn, sometimes even later if they escape early frosts, helping to bring color at a time when many border plants are past their best. Penstemons need a well-drained soil with plenty of sun, a regular supply of moisture during the growing season, and protection from winter cold (many are not reliably hardy).

FLOWER
SPIKE
8in (20cm)
long

BOUNTIFUL LADY
Although smaller than some other varieties, the purplish pink flowers of 'Catherine de la Mare' are produced in great profusion.

RED ALERT
The brilliant red flowers of 'Garnet' shine out in any border like the semiprecious gems after which they are named.

SOLO STAR
With its large, cerise-red flowers and clearly defined white throat, 'Maurice Gibbs' makes an impact, even when grown singly.

NOBLE PURPLE
The purple-red flowers of 'Countess of Dalkeith', each with a distinctive white throat, have considerable poise and elegance.

BLAZE OF GLORY, *right*
When grown among other late summer and early autumn flowers, 'Garnet' makes a dazzling and uninhibited trail of glowing red. As with all penstemons, regular deadheading will help prolong the flowering period.

For really small spaces, consider growing alpine penstemons, which are suited to troughs or in a rock garden.

Under ideal conditions, penstemons retain their foliage over the winter. However, don't worry if occasionally the foliage dies off — just remove it and watch for regrowth in spring.

GROWING
PENSTEMONS

PLANT PROFILE

Hardiness varies, so it is best to
treat most of them as tender
perennials. Most cultivars
Z 7–10; species Z 3–9.

- SIZE Most 2–3ft (60–90cm).
- FLOWER COLORS Red,
purple, lilac, pink, white,
cream.
- FLOWERING From mid-
summer to midautumn.
- SITE Well-drained soil, in
plenty of sun.

Cuttings None of the named
varieties can be raised from seed, so
buy new plants or take cuttings in
late summer and overwinter them
in a frost-free cold frame or
greenhouse. Plant out in late spring.

Soil A well-drained soil is essential.
If yours is heavy, dig in lots of sand
and compost to improve drainage,
and add extra sand to the planting
hole. Mulching helps conserve
moisture around roots in summer.

Protection Each winter, provide
individual plants with a loose, airy
layer of mulch, held in place with a
piece of chicken wire. In cold areas
or if a particularly severe winter is
forecast, either bring plants into a
frost-free cold frame or greenhouse,
or take cuttings in case the plant
does not survive.

My favorites 'Alice Hindley',
'Apple Blossom', *Penstemon barbatus*,
'Burgundy', 'Catherine de la Mare',
'Chester Scarlet', 'Countess of
Dalkeith', *P. digitalis* 'Albus',
'Firebird', 'Garnet', 'Maurice Gibbs',
'Osprey', 'Port Wine', 'Rubicundus',
'Sour Grapes', 'Stapleford Gem',
'White Bedder'.

TIMELESS ELEGANCE, *right*
The classic, elegant flowers of
'Stapleford Gem' are closely set
along the stems in subtle shades
of purple and pink. As with all
other penstemons, ensure that
the roots are kept moist, or the
number of flower spikes and the
length of the flowering period
will be reduced.

Lupines *LUPINUS*

ALTHOUGH LUPINES ARE classic cottage garden flowers, I find that they look just as at ease in a formal border as they do in a mixed border or informal planting. Above luxurious-looking mounds of light green, starlike leaves, the dense flowers form long-lasting spires of color for much of the summer. Although these hardy perennials are rather adaptable, they prefer, if possible, a slightly acidic soil and cool summers. Lupines will attract plenty of bees into your garden, especially on a warm, sunny day.

RAINBOW'S END, *above*
Available in a wide range of colors, the Russell Hybrids reliably produce cheerful hordes of densely packed flower spikes for a month or more.

SOLID COLOR
Choosing and grouping single-color lupines such as 'Chandelier' allows you to create strong blocks of color in a more coordinated border.

SPICE OF LIFE
Be bold and treat yourself to some of the more brightly colored lupines that are now available. Here, 'The Page', one o my passions, brings red-hot hues into your garden.

◄ FLOWER SPIKE
10in (25cm)
long

SMALL IS BEAUTIFUL, *left*
In smaller gardens or toward the front of the border, shorter varieties such as this gorgeous, richly colored dwarf Minarette Group lupine are especially useful.

MIX AND MATCH
Bicolored flowers, such as this pink and yellow Minarette, fascinate amateur lupine breeders and exhibition growers.

PERFECT HARMONY
Lupines have no great reputation for subtlety, but even the brashest colors can work in mixed plantings. Here, the pinkish red and white flowers of 'The Chatelaine' are easy on the eye among irises, ornamental alliums, and yarrow.

GROWING LUPINES

PLANT PROFILE
Annuals and perennials, usually surviving for a few years. Z 4–8.
- SIZE Most 30–42in (75–105cm).
- FLOWER COLORS Red, orange, yellow, blue, purple, lilac, pink, white, cream; many bicolors.
- FLOWERING Mostly summer; a few into early autumn.
- SITE Well-drained, neutral to acidic soil in sun or part shade.

Sowing seeds Sow seeds of annuals in open ground in spring. Perennials grown from seed need to spend their first year under glass.

Soil Improve drainage of heavy soil by adding plenty of sand or compost before planting, or choose a sloping site where drainage will be better. Do not overfeed.

Growing tip Remove the flower spike in the plant's first year; this will greatly increase vigor.

My favorites 'Chandelier', 'Dwarf Lulu', Gallery Series, 'Kayleigh Ann Savage', Minarette Group, 'My Castle', 'Noble Maiden', 'Pope John Paul', Russell Hybrids, ' The Chatelaine', 'The Governor', 'The Page'.

To save your own seed, cut off all but the lowest few whorls of faded flowers. Leaving the whole spike to develop seed will seriously weaken the plant, and the resultant seeds will be much smaller.

Named varieties do not come true from seed, so if you gather your own, be prepared for plenty of variation.

◄ FLOWER SPIKE
10in (25cm) long

Red-hot pokers *KNIPHOFIA*

I FIND RED-HOT POKERS more fascinating than beautiful, but there's no disputing that their proud, flame-colored flower spikes are absolute show-stoppers in a summer border. Sometimes also referred to as torch lilies, these perennials are surprisingly easy to grow in a sheltered spot in sun or part shade, and there are many different varieties to choose from in numerous shades of red, orange, yellow, cream, and bronze.

COOL CUSTOMER
The diminutive 'Little Maid' belies *Kniphofia*'s common name, with cool, milky yellow flowers on a dainty stem.

MORNING GLORY
For summertime echoes of a tequila sunrise, 'Bees' Sunset' is flushed orange to yellow down its flower stem.

WHITE HEAT
It may be called 'Strawberries and Cream', but to me this red-hot poker looks as if it has reached white-hot at the base!

GROWING RED-HOT POKERS

PLANT PROFILE
Perennials; they need a sheltered spot in regions with cold winters. Z 5–9.

- SIZE 2–5ft (60–150cm).
- FLOWER COLORS Red, orange, yellow, cream, bronze.
- FLOWERING The majority flower in midsummer.
- SITE Free-draining soil is especially important in winter. They prefer full sun but will do well in light shade.

Soil Red-hot pokers really do need well-drained soil. Don't let these otherwise easy plants suffer from winter moisture, or they will simply rot and die out.

Choosing plants By checking the flowering periods carefully before you buy you can, if you wish, have varieties coming into flower from one end of summer to the other.

Sowing seeds Sow seed of species and mixed varieties in autumn or spring. Grow seedlings on and transplant into flowering positions one year later. Seed-raised plants will need to be kept under glass until they are at least one year old. The more flamboyant red-hot pokers are the named varieties, which do not come true from seed.

Planting Incorporate sand in the planting hole and surrounding area if your soil is on the heavy side; this will decrease the likelihood of the plant rotting in winter.

Dividing Divide established plants carefully in either the autumn or spring. Unlike many other rhizomatous plants, red-hot pokers are not inclined to spread extensively and usually keep themselves growing in neat clumps.

Protection A mulch of straw, oak leaves, or other loose material is advisable to ensure that new plants survive their first couple of winters unscathed. Moisture is more likely to prove fatal than low temperatures. In cold areas, an annual mulch in autumn helps protect the crown in winter.

My favorites 'Alcazar', 'Bees' Sunset', *Kniphofia caulescens*, 'Cobra', 'Ice Queen', 'Little Maid', 'Samuel's Sensation', 'Toffee Nosed'.

GARDEN SIZZLERS
The warm, relaxing pinks and purples of this border that includes clematis, tamarisk, verbenas, and salvias are given a startling lift by the presence of a large clump of red-hot pokers.

FLOWER SPIKE ▶
8½in (22cm)
long

DYING EMBERS
As summer ends, red-hot pokers are slowly quenched from bottom to top. Dying flowers are not normally eye-catching, but in *Kniphofia linearifolia* the faded brown goes well with the still-vibrant red and orange.

If, despite your efforts, your red-hot pokers do not thrive, flower well, or even survive, and you suspect that your soil is too wet for them in winter, try replanting them on slight mounds to ensure that excess water drains away from around the base of the plants. You could also add garden sand to the soil to improve drainage. Water well in dry spells in the next summer.

TOWERING INFERNO
One of the classic red-hot pokers is 'Alcazar'. Its elongated, finger-like flowers bring a glowing warmth wherever you plant it.

Long stamens of bright yellow hang gracefully from open flowers

Verbascums *VERBASCUM*

THESE TALL, flower-decked columns are perfect for the middle or back of the border or in island beds. Verbascums also look lovely if allowed to self-seed and naturalize around the edge of a tree's canopy or in a wild garden, provided it is a reasonably sunny site. As well as their beautiful flower spikes, which attract crowds of bees, many have sumptuous, silvery, furry rosettes of foliage. As long as these perennials get lots of sunshine and, if possible, a poor, well-drained alkaline soil (these plants definitely do not like being fed too well), they will reward you with a bold display throughout the summer and often well into autumn.

OLYMPIAN HEIGHTS
One of the tallest and most imposing of the verbascums, *Verbascum olympicum* is often extensively branched toward the base of the flower spike, forming a fat plume.

DELICATE WHITES
The tall spikes of tiny white flowers of *Verbascum chaixii* 'Album' with contrasting mauve centers can be used to lighten flowers of many colors. The leaves are semievergreen.

PRETTY AS A PICTURE
The subtly colored flowers of *Verbascum chaixii* 'Gainsborough' remind me of primroses in spring. They produce a long-lasting display over a rosette of semievergreen foliage.

PRIMA DONNA
Throughout the summer, *Verbascum chaixii* 'Cotswold Queen' reigns supreme, producing unbranched spikes of bright yellow flowers with purple-brown centers.

GROWING VERBASCUMS

A SECOND GLANCE, *right*
'Helen Johnson' is one of the few "trendy" plants I've allowed myself to fall in love with, although I admit the pinkish brown flowers are an acquired taste.

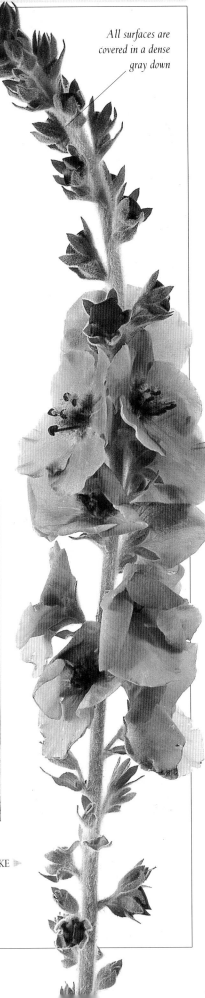

All surfaces are covered in a dense gray down

PLANT PROFILE

Biennials, perennials, and a few annuals. Less hardy varieties need winter protection. Z 5–9.

• SIZE 12–60in (30–150cm); most are 3–4ft (90–120cm).

• FLOWER COLORS Yellow, purple, lilac, pink, white, brown.

• FLOWERING Throughout summer and into autumn.

• SITE Ideally, a very poor and free-draining soil in full sun out of strong winds.

Raising plants Some verbascums can be raised from seed, but root cuttings are the best method for propagating named varieties. Take root cuttings, about 3in (7.5cm) long, in early spring. Root them in a mixture of half peat and half sand in a cold frame. Once the young plants have three or four leaves, pot them individually, then plant out in the flower bed in autumn. You can divide mature perennial varieties in spring.

Protection The less hardy varieties 'Golden Wings' and 'Letitia' and the species *Verbascum dumulosum* need a sheltered site and good drainage. If in doubt as to whether these can be provided, cover plants during winter to protect them from cold and moisture.

My favorites *V. bombyciferum*, *V. b.* 'Arctic Summer'; *V. chaixii* 'Album', *V. c.* 'Cotswold Beauty', *V. c.* 'Gainsborough', *V. c.* 'Pink Domino'; 'Helen Johnson'.

GRAY EMINENCE, *above*
The enormous, woolly, gray-leaved verbascums such as *Verbascum bombyciferum*, *V. chaixii* (nettle-leaved mullein), and *V. olympicum* form dramatic, architectural towers of foliage that add a spectacular focal point to the garden long before the first flower opens.

FLOWER SPIKE ▶
10in (25cm)
long

In the right conditions, most verbascums self-seed readily. They may not be true to type but are well worth keeping.

Foxgloves *DIGITALIS*

WHY SETTLE FOR a flat expanse of a plain groundcover under trees and large shrubs when you can accentuate vertical shafts of dappled sunlight with the palely glimmering, coolly elegant spires of foxgloves? Most bear their first and finest flowers in their second year, after which they are best replaced. However, foxgloves are formidable self-seeders and, provided that you are happy with a rather unpredictable mixture of flower shades in their offspring, will perpetuate themselves almost indefinitely.

SOLO PERFORMANCE
For a single-color effect the warm shades of 'Sutton's Apricot' are particularly hard to resist. The color fades as flowers open.

AN EASY FIT
The unassuming, delicate slipper-like flowers of *Digitalis grandiflora* are especially well suited to a wild or natural garden.

If you want to save seed from white foxgloves, grow the parent plants as far away as possible from foxgloves in other colors for the best chance of white-flowered seedlings. Alternatively, buy fresh seed every year.

All parts of the foxglove are dangerous if eaten, and contact with the foliage can irritate skin, so keep them away from small children playing in the garden.

◀ FLOWER SPIKE
24–30in
(60–75cm)
long

FAST AND FOXY, *above*
The Foxy hybrids of *Digitalis purpurea* may be sown outdoors in early spring and will usually be in flower by late summer of the same year.

WOODLAND IDYLL, *right*
Although they are equally at home in a sunny border, the dreamlike quality of foxgloves really comes through under the boughs of a spreading tree.

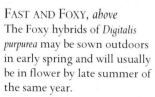

GROWING FOXGLOVES

PLANT PROFILE

Biennials and perennials.
Z 4–8.

- SIZE 18–60in (45–150cm).
- FLOWER COLORS Yellow, purple, lilac, pink, white, cream, brown.
- FLOWERING Early summer to early autumn.
- SITE Any soil will do, provided it is not too wet or too dry, in full sun or any but heavy shade.

Sowing seeds Sow direct outside in late spring or early summer for flowers in the following year.

Self-seeding As soon as self-sown seedlings beneath a plant are about 4in (10cm) tall they can be moved, if desired. Take a good trowelful of soil with the roots and keep very well watered after transplanting. Because foxgloves cross-pollinate very readily, offspring rarely look the same as the parent plants.

Siting Planted in a shady spot, a foxglove grows somewhat taller than if planted in sun, so bear this in mind when planning.

Support Provided they are neither overfed nor grown in an exposed site, staking should not be necessary.

Flower care If faded flower spikes are removed promptly, a new flush of flower spikes may develop, although usually much smaller.

My favorites *Digitalis ferruginea;* *D. grandiflora; D. laevigata* subsp. *graeca; D. lanata; D. lutea; D. × mertonensis; D. purpurea, D. p.* f. *albiflora, D. p.* Excelsior Group, *D. p.* Foxy Group, *D. p.* 'Sutton's Apricot' (sometimes called 'Apricot Beauty', or even just Apricot'); *D. viridiflora.*

A CUT ABOVE, *right*
This small hybrid foxglove, *Digitalis × mertonensis,* is especially good as a cut flower; like all other foxgloves, it is guaranteed to attract hosts of bees to your garden.

Hollyhocks *ALCEA ROSEA*

ALTHOUGH NINETEENTH-CENTURY artists often depicted hollyhocks standing bolt upright in tidy, picture-perfect cottage gardens, I must admit I like to leave mine unstaked in the more informal areas of my garden to flop as they will. For a more dramatic effect, they look striking lined up in a row next to the wall of a house or neatly staked around the edges of a vegetable plot. These sturdy biennials or perennials thrive in a heavy soil in full sun or in a slightly shaded position, but I've even seen a volunteer seedling growing from a crack in pavement.

MIXED BLESSINGS, *left*
Sow a packet of Single Mixed seed and you are guaranteed long-lasting, eye-catching flowers in tempting shades of purple, pink, white, cream, and yellow.

◄ FLOWER SIZE
2–4in (5–10cm) across

Flowers open in succession from the base of the spire to the tip

DOUBLE TAKE
With flowers like paper pompons, 'Chater's Double' and other double forms have a blowsier style from that of the single form.

BLACK BEAUTY
Why bother searching to find a black tulip when you can so easily have spikes of the gorgeous, silky-smooth, purple-black flowers of hollyhock 'Nigra'?

GROWING HOLLYHOCKS

PLANT PROFILE

Most are perennials or biennials. Provide winter protection in severely cold areas. Z 3–9.

- SIZE 4–8ft (1.2–2.4m).
- FLOWER COLORS Red, yellow, purple, lilac, pink, white, cream.
- FLOWERING Summer, sometimes into early autumn.
- SITE Heavy soil in full sun or part shade. Protect from strong winds.

Planting Add general fertilizer to the soil before planting, and feed throughout the summer. An annual autumn mulch of compost or well-rotted horse manure is beneficial.

Sowing seeds Sow seeds direct in summer or spring the year before the flowering plants are desired. If you can provide heat (55°F/13°C), you can sow seeds under glass in late winter. Harden them off and plant out in midspring for flowers that summer.

Protection Hollyhocks are very prone to a fungal rust disease that can devastate their foliage and seriously weaken the plants. Raising your own plants will ensure that they start out rust-free. Spray young and mature plants regularly with a suitable fungicide.

My favorites 'Chater's Double', in apricot or mixed; 'Majorette'; 'Nigra'; Single Mixed.

Hollyhock seeds are easy to gather, and, although they are unlikely to come true, you will still have beautiful flowers.

Single Mixed can flower along at least 3ft (90cm) of the stem

◀ FLOWER SIZE
3in (7.5cm) across

SITTING PRETTY
Hollyhocks look most at home in the cottage garden. Here, next to the branches of a deep purple buddleia, they make a striking wall of color.

OPEN SEASON, *right*
Behind each of the first flowers to open on a hollyhock spire is another plump green jewel of a flower bud waiting its turn – no wonder their display is so long-lasting.

Veronicas *VERONICA*

THE PIERCING BLUE OF classic veronicas – sometimes known as speedwells – is a refreshing sight in any sunny border and lasts from mid-spring to early summer. Less widely grown but equally easy to look after are the pink and white forms, which, like the blue veronicas, have a distinct central "eye" to each flower. Most are grown in borders, but some of the smaller varieties are best suited to a rock garden. Once established, veronicas will produce a bold block of color, though on close inspection the individual plants are delicate and fragile. They are simple to grow as long as they have plenty of sun and well-drained soil. Bees and butterflies find them irresistible.

OUT OF THE BLUE, *right*
Veronica spicata has produced varieties growing from 12 to 24in (30 to 60cm); shown here is one of the taller of the group.

Tiny individual flowers

GROWING VERONICAS

PLANT PROFILE

Perennials; varieties damaged by winter moisture should be protected. Z 4–8.

• SIZE 3–20in (7.5–50cm), but *Veronica longifolia* reaches a towering 6ft (1.8m).

• FLOWER COLORS Blue, pink, white.

• FLOWERING From mid-spring to early summer.

• SITE Well-drained, average soil in full sun or slight shade, sheltered from strong winds.

Planting Before planting on a very light or sandy soil, check that it contains a reasonable amount of organic matter. If not, incorporate leafmold or well-rotted compost before planting.

Dividing Divide established clumps in spring or autumn. Dividing every three years helps keep plants in good condition.

Cuttings Some species are too brittle to divide successfully. Take semiripe cuttings in midsummer, and root in a cold frame.

Sowing seeds Only the species can be raised from seed. Sow in early spring under glass, harden off, and put plants into their permanent positions in autumn.

Pruning Remove faded flowers or lightly trim the whole plant when flowering is over. This helps keep plants compact and encourages better flowering the following year.

Protection *Veronica bombycina* is damaged by cold and wet conditions over winter so is best avoided unless you have a suitable greenhouse.

Support In exposed positions or for plants grown in part shade, you may need to give them some support. Twiggy branches are best – thick stakes may damage delicate stems.

My favorites *Veronica austriaca* 'Crater Lake Blue'; *V. longifolia*; *V. peduncularis* 'Georgia Blue'; *V. prostrata*; *V. p.* 'Rosea'; *V. spicata*; 'Sunny Border Blue'; *V. virginica* (sometimes known as *Veronicastrum virginicum*). For very dry conditions, try *V. gentianoides*.

COLOR CONTRAST, *above*
The yellow-green foliage of
the low-growing *Veronica
prostrata* 'Trehane'
provides a strong
background for
the spikes of
blue flowers.

FLOWER SPIKE ▶
12in (30cm)
long

LOFTY ELEGANCE
One of the taller
veronicas, *Veronica
virginica* 'Rosea' often
grows to over 6ft
(1.8m) and is topped with
surprisingly slender
spikes of delicate, pale
pink flowers.

*Tubular flowers
with protruding
stamens*

*Flowers open
in succession
toward the tip*

*In moist ground, grow
Veronica beccabunga, which
thrives in boggy conditions.*

*The low-growing V. cinerea is
ideal as a groundcover. Each
plant forms a mat of woody
stems 12in (30cm) in diameter.*

*V. peduncularis forms a mat
of bright blue flowers, ideal for
growing in between stones.*

PURPLE HAZE
The pretty, lilac-blue spikes of
Veronica longifolia remind me of a
miniature version of buddleia.
They appear from late summer
to early autumn.

FLAT OUT
This mat-forming *Veronica spicata*
'Rotfuchs' grows to only about
12in (30cm) high but seems larger
than life when it breaks out into
masses of zingy pink flowers.

THINK PINK
With its elegant whorls of languid leaves and its very slim, tapering
flower clusters, this pale pink *Veronica virginica* is a real gem in
midsummer, when pastel colors can be scarce.

Bold & beautiful

IN FLORAL SOCIAL CIRCLES THEY MAY BE INSUFFERABLE, BUT I LOVE HAVING A FEW REAL SHOWOFFS IN THE GARDEN. ALL FLOWERS ARE LOVELY, TO BE SURE, BUT THE ONES I'VE CHOSEN here really flaunt their attributes — these are no shrinking violets! All but one of my choices are classic beauties, from statuesque lilies to positively Rubenesque peonies. Some — for example, sweet peas — advertise their voluptuous charms still further with heady perfume, too. Euphorbias might be considered to be imposters in the camp, for their showy "flowers" are in reality conspicuous, brightly colored leafy bracts, and the tiny and very modest flower in the center of each often goes unnoticed. Nevertheless, I make no apology for including these truly unusual plants; I find their shape and color both beautiful and utterly fascinating.

> *"Although their exquisitely silky blooms don't last long, I couldn't bear to miss my annual brief romance with peonies."*
>
> PEONIES, PAGES 54—55

Left IRISES (PP.60—61), AMONG THE MOST STRIKING AND ELEGANT PLANTS IN THE BORDER

49

Alliums *ALLIUM*

IT'S HARD TO BELIEVE that these close relatives of the humble onion can be so striking. Onions going to seed have flowers that are a lovely shape but are a rather dull and dirty cream; paint them in bright colors, and their exquisite form shouts for attention. Grow these bulbous perennials to create tall exclamation marks in a border, or use dwarf varieties to make a carpet of color in summer. I like to grow alliums in weathered terracotta pots, although wherever I put them I still expect to see a row of cabbages nearby, too!

Pompons are made up of star-shaped flowers

CELESTIAL BLUE
Clusters of powder blue star-shaped flowers densely grouped together give *Allium caeruleum* a soft, dreamy look.

HOT PINK
Commonly known as the nodding onion, *Allium cernuum* has deep pink, bell-like flowers on exaggerated arching stems.

STAR TURN, *right*
This dazzling sphere of color is *Allium aflatunense* 'Purpureum', with tightly packed, star-shaped flowers of rich pink tinged with purple.

WHITE ON WHITE, *above*
When in flower, *Allium stipitatum* 'Album' creates a wonderful show of white and cream pompons. The faded flowerheads left in the border look handsome sparkling in heavy frost – or bring them indoors to use in dried flower arrangements.

PURPLE DRIFT, *left*
This loose planting of the purplish pink *Allium aflatunense* reminds me of brightly colored hats in a bustling crowd. Close planting with Jacob's ladder (*Polemonium*) in purple and white, herbaceous geraniums, and the pinkish white flowerheads of London pride (*Saxifraga* × *urbium*) add to the informal air of this border.

Sturdy stems make alliums particularly good for cutting

GROWING ALLIUMS

PLANT PROFILE

Bulbs that flower every year: some benefit from protection during cold winters. Z 4–9.

- SIZE 12–48in (30–120cm).
- FLOWER COLORS Yellow, blue, purple, lilac, pink, white.
- FLOWERING From midspring to well into autumn.
- SITE Fertile, well-drained soil in full sun is essential for most; incorporate sand on planting to improve drainage.

Planting Plant bulbs 2–4in (5–10cm) deep in mid- to late autumn.

Dividing Congested clumps can be divided in autumn or spring.

Support Tall plants may need staking in exposed gardens.

Plant care Unless you are saving them for drying, remove the flowerheads as soon as they have faded. The stems and foliage should be left on the plant until they die, when they can be removed.

My favorites *Allium aflatunense*, *A. caeruleum*, *A. cernuum*, *A. flavum*, *A. giganteum*, *A. karataviense*, *A. neapolitanum*, *A. oreophilum* (syn. *A. ostrowskianum*), *A. sphaerocephalon*, *A. unifolium*. For naturalizing under shrubs, *A. moly* and *A. triquetrum* are both good. *A. cristophii* has flowerheads up to 8in (20cm) in diameter and is among the best for winter decoration.

For scent, grow Allium triquetrum, *whose white and green-striped flowers appear in midspring. It can be very invasive; for something less aggressive try* A. cowanii, *which produces white flowers in mid- to late spring.*

Dried allium seedheads make superb additions to dried flower arrangements. As the flowers fade, cut the stems using sharp scissors and hang them upside down in small bunches in a well-ventilated room.

The spidery, six-pointed flowers have an almost metallic look to them

FLOWERHEAD ▶
8in (20cm)
across

DRAMA QUEEN
The outlandishly large, globe-like flowerheads of *Allium cristophii* draw attention to themselves in any garden, large or small. They spring up as if from nowhere and soon tower above their companions, grabbing attention away from all but the boldest flowers.

Flattened flowers provide easy access for bees

Euphorbias *EUPHORBIA*

WEIRD AND WONDERFUL, euphorbias make you either shudder or swoon – and although I admit I was once in the former camp, they're now one of my favorite architectural plants, as much for their showy petal-like bracts as for their sheer versatility. Despite their extraordinary, almost surreal appearance they are surprisingly easy to combine with other plants. Most of them are perennials and are happy in a wide range of conditions. They provide a really distinctive show from midspring right up until late summer.

FIRE BRIGHT
You couldn't find a better name than 'Fireglow' for this *Euphorbia griffithii*, with its smoldering orange-red bracts and red leaf veins.

ALL CHANGE
Like its namesake, *Euphorbia dulcis* 'Chameleon', with its rich purple leaves, blends in magically with surrounding colors in any shade of purple, red, or green.

RAZZLE DAZZLE
Although the individual bracts of *Euphorbia palustris* are comparatively small, they are produced in such quantity that they create a mass of bright yellow.

The milky sap of euphorbias is a skin irritant, so take care when cutting back plants; wear gloves and long sleeves. If the sap comes into contact with your skin, wash it off immediately. Seek medical advice if you get the sap in your eyes. Avoid planting euphorbias near a pond that contains fish, since the fish may react adversely to the sap.

LEMON ZEST
The lemon-lime bracts of *Euphorbia polychroma* bring an intense and unusual splash of color from mid-spring to late summer.

◄ FLOWER SIZE
1¼in (3cm) across

GROWING EUPHORBIAS

PLANT PROFILE

Mainly perennials, although others are annual, biennial, or shrubby. Z 4–9.

- SIZE 12–60in (30–150cm).
- FLOWER COLORS Red, orange, yellow, green.
- FLOWERING From mid-spring to late summer.
- SITE Prefer well-drained soil in sun but will tolerate a wide range of soils and part shade.

Planting To get euphorbias off to a good start, add well-rotted compost to increase soil fertility.

Dividing Divide mature plants in spring or autumn. *Euphorbia polychroma* has a very woody crown, so lift the whole plant and cut it into sections using a knife or spade. You can also increase your plant stock from seed (sow seeds in spring in a cold frame), or take basal shoot cuttings in late spring and root in a cold frame.

Growing tip Most euphorbias will produce a second flush of growth if cut back hard after flowering and kept well watered and fed.

My favorites *Euphorbia amygdaloides* var. *robbiae*; *E. characias* subsp. *characias* 'Humpty Dumpty', *E. c.* subsp. *wulfenii*, *E. c.* subsp. *w.* 'Lambrook Gold', *E. c.* subsp. *w.* 'Spring Splendour'; *E. dulcis* 'Chameleon'; *E. polychroma*. For a moist, shady site or even a bog garden, *E. griffithii* 'Dixter' and *E. g.* 'Fireglow' are ideal. As a groundcover in light shade, try *E. polychroma* 'Candy' (syn. 'Purpurea').

OUT OF THIS WORLD, *right* One of the strangest and the most striking looking of the euphorbias is *Euphorbia characias* subsp. *wulfenii*. In no time at all this evergreen biennial produces a mass of blue-green whorls of foliage topped by large domes of yellow-green bracts.

Peonies *PAEONIA*

HERBACEOUS PEONIES bring fleeting but unashamed luxury to the garden. Although their exquisitely silky blooms don't last very long, I couldn't bear to miss my annual brief romance with peonies – and their attractively divided foliage earns its ornamental keep for the rest of the season. Peonies, especially the deep pink or red form of *Paeonia officinalis*, form an integral part of any cottage-garden-style planting. The young foliage often has a pinkish tinge to it and looks superb emerging close to crown imperials (*Fritillaria imperialis*). Alternatively, try underplanting with the small snakeshead fritillaries, miniature daffodils, crocuses, or grape hyacinths.

DREAM TICKET
The closely packed, paper-thin pale pink petals of 'Sarah Bernhardt' would fulfill any little girl's fantasy of possessing a silken petticoat skirt fit for a fairy-tale princess.

BOWLED OVER
The wonderful creamy-colored center of 'Bowl of Beauty' is surrounded by a collar of shell-like pink petals.

WHITE GOLD
With a deep bowl of white around a dense mound of rich golden stamens, 'Krinkled White' is almost waterlily-like in beauty.

PINK FLUSH
The semidouble flowers of 'Auguste Dessert' have unusual bright pink petals, each one streaked with a darker pink.

ROYAL STANDARD
I love to grow deep red peonies such as *Paeonia tenuifolia*; their central boss of golden stamens stands out with a regal air.

GROWING PEONIES

PLANT PROFILE

These are long-lived perennials. For taller plants, consider the shrubby tree peonies. Z 3–8.
- SIZE Most 2–3ft (60–90cm).
- FLOWER COLORS Red, pink, white, cream.
- FLOWERING Early summer.
- SITE Moisture-retentive yet well-drained soil, in full sun. Provide shade from early-morning sun following a frosty night.

Planting Incorporate plenty of well-rotted compost when planting. Do not bury the crowns more than 1in (2.5cm) beneath the surface, or flowering will be reduced.

Dividing Divide established crowns in autumn, but only if really necessary; they resent disturbance.

Flowering Keep plants well watered and feed with balanced fertilizer in spring and autumn.

Pruning Deadhead as soon as flowers fade. Cut back to the ground in autumn.

Wilting If stems blacken at the base and then wilt, the fungal infection peony wilt is probably to blame. Remove all affected stems completely as soon as they are seen, cutting right back into the crown if necessary.

My favorites 'America', 'Bowl of Beauty', 'Coral Charm', 'Duchesse de Nemours', 'Félix Crousse', 'Festiva Maxima', 'Karl Rosenfield', 'Laura Dessert', 'Lize van Veen', 'Nellie Saylor', 'Pillow Talk', 'Président Poincaré', 'Sarah Bernhardt', 'Scarlett o'Hara', *Paeonia officinalis* 'Alba Plena', *P. o.* 'Rosea Plena', *P. o.* 'Rubra Plena'.

Use ring stakes, bamboo stakes, or twiggy branches to support tall-growing peonies, especially those that are in exposed sites.

Stems and leaves are often flushed with pink or red

Petals have slightly wavy edges or are indented

FLOWER SIZE ▶
4in (10cm)
across

PRINCE CHARMING
You might be forgiven for mistaking 'Arabian Prince' for a confectioner's exotic creation! With its screaming pink petals and rich yellow stamens, this peony demands attention wherever it is planted.

GOOD COMPANIONS, *right*
Peonies are wonderful plants for herbaceous and mixed borders, where they can be combined easily with a wide range of perennials, shrubs, or climbers. Nearly all of them make marvelous companions for other showy flowers such as roses, delphiniums, and alliums.

Sweet peas *LATHYRUS ODORATUS*

THEY MAY BE AS SUBTLE as a carnival ride, but many people will happily own up to a weakness for sweet peas. And why not? If you are not seduced by their frilly, butterfly-like flowers in the loveliest colors imaginable, then you will be by their fetching perfume. These fast-growing annual climbers are easy to raise from seed and will create a quick screen, clothe a tepee, or brighten up a shrub throughout the summer in cooler areas.

Delicate tendrils for attachment

SCENTED HEAVEN
With its heavily scented, bluish mauve flowers, 'Noel Sutton' is a favorite for which I can always find a place.

Elegantly winged stems

PURE AND SIMPLE
The pure white, lightly perfumed flowers of 'White Supreme' make long-lasting, elegant cut flowers.

OLD AND NEW
The bright, rose-pink flowers of 'Jayne Amanda' look equally good in a modern or traditional cottage garden.

OF CABBAGES AND KINGS
This sweet pea was picked fresh from my garden. I like to grow them among the vegetables so that I can harvest crops and flowers together.

FLOWER SIZE ▶
1½in (3.5cm) long

GROWING SWEET PEAS

PLANT PROFILE
Annual climbers. A few make low mounds.

• SIZE 36in (90cm) is average; tall ones reach 6–10ft (1.8–3m), dwarf just 6–12in (15–30cm).

• FLOWER COLORS Red, orange, yellow, purple, lilac, pink, white, cream.

• FLOWERING Late spring into summer.

• SITE Moist, fertile soil, in full sun or part shade.

Soil Preparing the ground before sowing or planting is essential. The soil must be kept constantly moist if sweet peas are to continue to flower throughout the season. Dig in plenty of organic matter, such as well-rotted horse manure or compost, to encourage soil moisture retention. Mulch to keep soil cool.

Sowing seeds Sow seed in mid-autumn or early spring. The seed coats of the black or mottled seeds are tough, so germination is more reliable and quick if you nick the seed coat opposite the "eye" first. Seeds can be sown either in pots or trays or in special sweet pea tubes (these allow you to grow the plants on and transplant them with minimum root disturbance). To encourage good, bushy growth, pinch out the growing tips of the seedlings once they have two pairs of leaves. Harden off and plant out in mid- to late spring.

Watering Regular watering is the key to success. Good soil preparation will make this an easier task, but even then sweet peas need plenty of moisture if they are to flower constantly and for the maximum possible length of time.

Plant problems Sweet peas are prone to a range of fungal diseases that build up in the soil, so always choose a fresh site every year.

Support Most sweet peas must have some support. Their tendrils will cling to netting, wires, stakes, twiggy branches, or shrubs.

My favorites 'Blue Mantle', 'Cambridge Blue', 'Catherine', 'Charles Unwin', 'Daphne', 'Diamond Wedding', 'Midnight', 'Milestone', 'Noel Sutton', 'Old Times', 'Painted Lady', 'Patio Mixed', 'Pulsar', 'White Supreme'.

High Climbers, *above*

For a simple yet attractive feature, grow sweet peas up a frame of twiggy sticks or stakes in the border or, if space is limited, in a container, where they will quickly create a mass of color.

Mixed Medley, *right*

Sweet peas come in pastel or dark shades, pure colors, or bicolors to suit all tastes. They look charming when many colors are grown together.

Sowing in individual tall pots keeps root disturbance to a minimum when planting. Better still, choose paper or fiber pots that disintegrate in the soil.

Tulips *TULIPA*

THE NATURAL Less showy than many of the cultivated varieties, *Tulipa kurdica* produces a subtle, natural-looking display.

THE DAYS OF "TULIP MANIA" may be over, but using tulips is still a splendid way to create a bright splash of color early in the year. They come in a wide range of shapes and colors to suit every whim and location. Tulips are often thought of as too much bother, because it is best to plant new bulbs every year for the showiest display. However, it is often worth experimenting and leaving them in the ground; some may reappear for several years. *Tulipa kaufmanniana* is one of the more reliable repeat performers.

AMONG CHAMPIONS The bright yellow petals of 'Olympic Flame' are streaked orange-red; they look great with other red or yellow flowers.

HIDDEN VIRTUES, *right* Forget-me-nots (*Myosotis*) go well with many tulips. As an added bonus, the foliage masks the tulip leaves as they age and fade.

MYSTIQUE OF THE EAST Tulip petals have beautiful textures; the silky, pale purple petals of 'Arabian Mystery' are edged in delicate white lace.

GROWING TULIPS

PLANT PROFILE

Not reliably perennial, but many kinds will reappear for at least a few years. Z 4–7.

• SIZE 4–30in (10–75cm).

• FLOWER COLORS Red, orange, yellow, green, purple, lilac, pink, white, cream.

• FLOWERING Spring.

• SITE Light or medium well-drained soil in sun or part shade, ideally in a sheltered position.

Planting Varies with bulb size, but usually about 6in (15cm) deep. On sandy soils, plant bulbs even deeper than this. To make formal-looking blocks of color, plant the bulbs only 4in (10cm) apart and in straight rows. Plant in midautumn, no earlier. This will greatly reduce the risk of them succumbing to tulip fire, a disfiguring and potentially fatal fungal disease.

Lifting You can plant bulbs in open-sided baskets (e.g. pond baskets) or mesh bags so that they can be lifted easily at the end of flowering. Allow the foliage to die back before storing.

Forcing Many tulips may be grown in pots for early spring bloom. Plant in autumn, keep moist in a cold (40°F/4°C) place for at least 12 weeks, then gradually expose to light and heat.

My favorites 'Apeldoorn', 'Apricot Beauty', 'Attila', 'Ballerina', 'Cassini', 'Estella Rijnveld', *T. fosteriana, T. kaufmanniana, T. kurdica,* 'Olympic Flame', 'Orange Emperor', 'Oxford', Parrot Group, 'Queen of Night', 'Red Emperor', 'Red Riding Hood', *T. saxatilis,* 'Scarlet Baby', 'Shirley', 'Showwinner', *T. sprengeri,* 'Stresa', 'Toronto', 'Waterlily'.

At the end of the season as the foliage yellows you can lift tulips, loosen off soil, and store in a cool place until autumn.

REGAL FLAME
The flowers of 'Orange Monarch' have a fiery glow, but look inside and you will see purple anthers set against apricot-orange petals.

TWIST AND SHOUT
Love them or hate them, the crazy flowers of Parrot tulips are always eye-catching, as the bright, frilly 'Flaming Parrot' proves.

ATTILA THE HONEY
The purple-pink blooms of 'Attila' may be very simple, but their elegance and sheer prettiness makes them a favorite with me.

GOLD STANDARD
If you want to grow a truly classic tulip, try 'Golden Apeldoorn'. It is taller than most; peek inside to see the black bases of the petals.

DARK STAR
The lovely, deep maroon flowers of 'Queen of Night' make me wonder why people still search for the elusive black tulip.

BABY LOVE, *right*
Planted *en masse*, the low-growing 'Scarlet Baby' creates a stunning display.

FLOWER SIZE ▶
3in (7.5cm)
across

PRETTY IN PINK, *above*
'Angélique' is among the most popular of tulips, although at first glance you might think that it is a peony!

59

Irises *IRIS*

IRIS WAS THE GREEK GODDESS of the rainbow, and there are irises across the entire color spectrum to justify that name. Bearded irises have a beardlike cluster of hairs on their lower petals; beardless irises are "clean-shaven." You can grow irises almost anywhere in the garden; although many need a free-draining, sunny position, some, such as the Siberian irises, do very well in a moist spot in light shade. Many irises bloom in the gap between spring and summer, providing color before summer borders come into their own.

BARE-FACED BRILLIANCE, *above*
'Shirley Pope', a Siberian iris, is beardless – as you might well expect from her name! I've always loved this classic iris.

Try to control slugs and snails around irises since their feeding damage may encourage the development of rhizome soft rot, a potentially fatal iris disease.

Iris leaves may be marred by pale brown spotting due to fungal leaf spot disease. This usually begins to develop in spring, especially in warm, wet weather. If the problem is severe, spray with a suitable fungicide.

HEIGHT OF FASHION
Between late spring and the start of summer the tall, demure, pink-lilac iris 'Carnaby' stands nearly waist high in the border.

LOWER THE FLAG
Perfect for smaller gardens or toward the front of a border, the miniature tall bearded iris 'Joette' is half the height of 'Carnaby'.

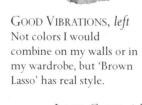

GOOD VIBRATIONS, *left*
Not colors I would combine on my walls or in my wardrobe, but 'Brown Lasso' has real style.

INNER GLOW, *right*
If you can position irises so that their petals are backlit by the sun, they will take on a translucence that suggests that they are glowing from within.

FLOWER SIZE ▶
4–5in (10–13cm)
across

GROWING IRISES

PLANT PROFILE

Perennials. Mostly Z 4–8.

- SIZE Most 10–36in (25–90cm).
- FLOWER COLORS An enormous range of colors and combinations.
- FLOWERING Most mid-spring to early or midsummer.
- SITE Many prefer sandy or free-draining loam in full sun. Others do well in moist soil in part shade or sun.

Planting Plant rhizomes in late summer or autumn. If possible, dig in some very well-rotted organic matter; do this several weeks before planting or not at all. Space rhizomes to allow for spread, with the surface of each rhizome *just* below ground level with the leaves facing the sun to ensure maximum exposure to sunlight. Trim back any leaves by about half to reduce the risk of wind rock loosening the young roots. Keep the rhizomes well watered for a couple of weeks after planting to encourage establishment. Feed in late autumn with a balanced fertilizer, alfalfa pellets, superphosphate, or bonemeal.

Dividing Divide bearded irises about 6–10 weeks after bloom; beardless generally in late summer or early autumn.

My favorites Bearded: 'Ask Alma', 'Bumblebee Deelite', 'Conjuration', 'Cotton Blossom', 'Dusky Challenger', 'Feed Back', 'Hot Spice', 'Jesse's Song', 'Joyce Terry', 'Lemon Mist', 'Mary Frances', 'Pele', 'Red Zinger', 'Rosemary's Dream', 'Stepping Out', 'Vanity'. Siberian: 'Cambridge', 'Jewelled Crown', 'Shirley Pope', 'White Swirl'. Also *I. cristata*, *I. pseudacorus*, 'Roy Davidson'.

BRONZED ADONIS, *right*
Striking plants of great stature, irises merit close examination to appreciate the fine detailed markings and color finishes of petals. Here, 'Bronze Cloud' takes on almost rainbowlike colors.

Lilies *LILIUM*

WHETHER GROWING in a border or container, lilies always look elegant, stately, and perhaps just a tiny bit aloof. Their striking good looks, often combined with a powerful scent, make them a real favorite. They are easy to grow if given well-drained soil and a little (but not too much) shade. Even if you are restricted to a backyard or balcony, you can fill it with the intense colors and scents of lilies, since many of them thrive in pots.

HEAVENLY TRUMPETS
The delicious fragrance of *Lilium longiflorum* is paradisical. Add to this its elegant flowers, and it's close to perfection!

QUEEN OF LILIES
With its heady perfume and striking purple or purple-brown markings, *Lilium regale* deserves a prominent position.

PEAK OF PERFECTION
I love the texture of pale lily petals; those of 'Mont Blanc' look like satiny slopes of whipped cream.

CRIMSON CUPS
Place a pot or two of the dazzling 'Red Night' in the early summer border to bring a color scheme to life.

GROWING LILIES

PLANT PROFILE

Bulbs that flower every year: deeply mulch marginally hardy lilies over winter. Z3–8.

• SIZE 2–4ft (60–120cm); some up to 10ft (3m).

• FLOWER COLORS Red, orange, yellow, purple, lilac, pink, white, cream, brown.

• FLOWERING Early, mid- or late summer.

• SITE Fertile soil; part shade or sun, depending on variety.

Planting Early spring, or autumn to flower the following summer. Bulbs establish better if soaked in water for an hour before planting. It's important to plant deep enough, especially stem-rooting lilies – *Lilium longiflorum, L. martagon, L. regale*. Dig in plenty of well-rotted manure or compost to a depth of at least 8in (20cm), then plant the bulbs 4–6in (10–15cm) deep. Plant *L. candidum* and *L. cernuum* more shallowly, in about 2in (5cm) of soil.

Soil Rich but well-drained. Lilies are heavy feeders, so add plenty of compost or well-rotted manure, or

use a balanced fertilizer. Wet soil conditions, especially in a poorly drained container, cause the bulbs to die off rapidly, so make sure that drainage is very good. In clay soil, set bulbs on a layer of sharp sand 1in (2.5cm) deep.

Watering Although lilies cannot bear wet feet, they need a steady supply of moisture throughout the growing period, so regular watering is essential when the weather is dry.

Dividing Established clumps of lilies should be divided every three to five years.

Container growing Most lilies do well in pots: try 'Casablanca', 'Pink Perfection', 'Mont Blanc', *Lilium speciosum* var. *album*, or 'Red Carpet'. Three bulbs per 10–12in (25–30cm) pot of a soil-based mix works well. Drainage must be good, so make sure the mix is loose and the drainage hole is large.

My favorites 'African Queen', *Lilium candidum,* 'Casablanca', 'Connecticut King', 'Enchantment', *L. lancifolium,* 'Liberation', *L. longiflorum,* 'Magic Pink', *L. martagon,* 'Mont Blanc', 'Red Night', *L. regale,* 'Star Gazer' – to be honest, I like most lilies

Most lilies are quite hardy, but
some, like Lilium longiflorum
(above), can be harmed by cold.
If grown in containers, move to a
frost-free position over winter.

RED-HOT CHILI, *right*
The dashing 'Acapulco' has a
powerful fragrance to match its
striking red blooms. Here, it adds
a touch of spice to a border of
purples and pinks, which includes
roses, foxgloves, irises, veronicas,
cosmos, bleeding hearts, and
columbines. Try to position scented
varieties where you can enjoy the
full benefit of their perfume: on or
next to a terrace or patio or by a
garden seat, arbor, open window, or
frequently used path.

A STAR IS BORN, *left*
With almost no effort at all, the
red-flushed 'Star Gazer' can be a
real hit in midsummer. It's great in
containers, has a delicate fragrance,
and, like most lilies, it makes
an excellent cut flower.

Many lilies
have delicately
patterned petals

Take care that lily pollen
does not get onto fabrics
— the stain is difficult
to remove

FLOWER SIZE ▶
7in (18cm)
across

Taller varieties may need
some support, particularly
in exposed sites

Distinctive stamens come
in a range of contrasting
and complementary hues

Feathery & light

PICTURE SUMMER SKIES STUDDED WITH WISPS OF FEATHER-LIGHT CLOUDS . . . IT MUST BE MORE THAN COINCIDENCE THAT WHENEVER I WANT TO CREATE DREAMY DRIFTS OF COLOR, I NEARLY always think of flowers in shades of blue, mauve, and white, often with blue-gray tinted foliage. The flowers in this section are themselves mostly quite small, but it is not their individual form, size, or color that make them so worthwhile. By all means enjoy their demure, delicate features close up, but they truly come into their own when grown en masse, forming a billowing haze that is lovely in its own right or when it is used to link flowers with stronger colors and forms in a subtle, easy manner. Some, in particular cornflowers and nigellas, are ideal where you need some temporary, light "fillers" while permanent plants become established.

"At the height of summer, nigellas form a haze of vivid blues and purples, taking the heat out of the flower border."

NIGELLAS, PAGES 72—73

Left NIGELLAS (PP.72—73), BRINGING CLOUDS OF SOFT BLUE TO THE SUMMER BORDER

Cornflowers CENTAUREA

I CAN'T THINK of a more perfect cross between a wild and a cultivated flower than cornflowers. They are such a quick and easy way to bring a bright splash of color to a border or container, and many perennial forms are terrific values, flowering from early to midsummer and then producing a second flush of blooms in autumn. Even when they are not in flower, their foliage, which is often silvery gray, acts as a foil for other plants close by.

BLACK AND WHITE
With its prominent dark stamens and fine feathery petals, *Centaurea montana alba* combines great sturdiness with a fragile elegance.

PINK POMPON
Some cornflowers have very densely packed petals that form tight rosettes, such as this *Centaurea cyanus* 'Tall Rose', an unusual pink form.

SUMMER HEAT
Cornflowers with pinkish colors, such as this carmine *Centaurea dealbata* 'Steenbergii', will instantly bring a warm glow to any border or planting.

WHITE RELIEF
Delicate white markings, either frilling the edges of the petals or, as here with *Centaurea cyanus*, brightening up their bases, are characteristic of cornflowers.

INTO THE BLUE, *right*
Centaurea cyanus looks at its most striking when it is planted closely together to produce a mass of brilliant blue. Like all cornflowers, it makes a pretty cut flower.

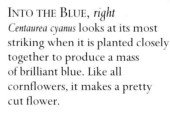

WILL O' THE WISP
Centaurea montana 'Pasham's Purple' has a timeless grace, with its very slender, pink-lilac petals and intricately patterned sepals.

GROWING CORNFLOWERS

PLANT PROFILE

Annuals, biennials, and perennials. Z 3–8.

- SIZE Most grow 8–18in (20–45cm); some varieties may reach 3ft (90cm).
- FLOWER COLORS Red, yellow, blue, purple, lilac, pink, white.
- FLOWERING From early summer to autumn.
- SITE Any well-drained soil, in full sun.

Sowing annuals Sow seeds of annuals direct into the ground in early autumn or early to midspring. Make several sowings throughout the spring to ensure a display of flowers for several months.

Growing perennials Sow seeds of perennials in spring, in pots or trays in a cold frame. Prick out, pot on, then plant in a spare piece of ground outside until autumn, when they should be ready to be planted in the border. You can divide mature plants about every three years, take cuttings, or buy small plants if you want to make a head start.

Soil Cornflowers will grow in any well-drained soil, as long as it is kept fertile. On heavy sites it is worth incorporating plenty of coarse sand or even planting on a slight mound to ensure better drainage.

Position Make sure that the site is sunny; without enough sunlight, flowering will be poor and the plants will become leggy.

My favorites *Centaurea cineraria*, *C. cyanus*, *C. hypoleuca* 'John Coutts', *C. macrocephala*, *C. montana alba*, *C. moschata* (syn. *Amberboa moschata*), 'Pulchra Major' (syn. *Leuzea centauroides*).

If you want to encourage wildlife, cornflowers are ideal, attracting both bees and butterflies into the garden.

•

Grow the mat-forming Centaurea bella in a sunny spot and you will be able to enjoy a silver-gray carpet of foliage topped with bright pinkish lilac flowers from late spring to midsummer.

Tiny petals are packed closely together to form little mopheads

FIELD OF DREAMS
Here, vibrant blue cornflowers look superb combined with godetia and California poppies in bright, contrasting shades of pink and orange.

◄ FLOWER SIZE
1½in (4cm)
across

Intricately patterned spherical buds

Sea hollies *ERYNGIUM*

IF THERE IS ONE PLANT that could conceivably have come from another planet, it's sea holly – the flowerheads really do look like outlandish spacecraft. All of them have a bright, almost metallic coloration to their leaves, stems, flowers, and spiky bracts. Most are herbaceous, a few are evergreen, and all flower constantly for most of the summer. They are an easy way to bring fast-growing color and really unusual texture and form into the garden. Given plenty of sun and a well-drained soil, they thrive and need very little attention.

TRUE STEEL
The vibrant, glistening, steely blue of *Eryngium alpinum* brings a metallic sheen to the border. To intensify the color, try underplanting with purples and blues.

TREASURE FROM THE DEEP
The flowers of *Eryngium variifolium* look as if they have been dried, however fresh they are. Their silvery, spiderlike appearance reminds me of a deep-sea creature.

SPIKY SOUVENIR
Eryngium gigateum is sometimes called Miss Willmott's Ghost. It appeared mysteriously in every garden that this great plantswoman visited; she was suspected of scattering seed.

GROWING SEA HOLLIES

PLANT PROFILE

Perennials and a few biennials. Z 3–9.

• SIZE Most 2–5ft (60–150cm); *Eryngium pandanifolium* will grow to a lofty 8ft (2.4m).

• FLOWER COLORS Green, blue, purple, lilac.

• FLOWERING Throughout the summer.

• SITE Ideally, well-drained soil and plenty of sun.

Soil Sea hollies will survive in all but the heaviest soils, but to thrive they need good drainage. When planting, work handfuls of coarse sand into the planting area if your soil is not very free-draining.

Position Without plenty of sun their growth becomes spindly and their metallic colors turn dull.

Sowing seed Some sea hollies can be raised from seed. Sow in spring, then plant out in autumn.

Cuttings Take root cuttings (see p.41) in late winter.

Dividing You can divide large plants in the autumn or spring.

Protection Cold, damp conditions over winter can kill these otherwise tough plants by encouraging rotting of the crown. Clearing all plant debris from the crown in autumn and mulching with a light, dry material such as pine needles will help stop rot on a less than perfect site.

Drying The flowerheads are striking in dried indoor arrangements and are best gathered on a dry day and suspended in a well-ventilated place to dry.

Planting partners Early spring bulbs such as crocuses make excellent companions for sea hollies. The bulbs will have finished flowering by the time the sea hollies have started, so neither plant cramps the other's style. Once the sea hollies have put on growth, they look stunning close to flowers with blue or lilac coloring, or a contrasting white.

My favorites *Eryngium agavifolium; E. alpinum; E. bourgatii, E. b.* 'Oxford Blue'; *E. giganteum; E. maritimum; E. × ol* *iverianum; E. proteiflorum; E. × tripartitum; E. variifolium.*

Prominent gray-white veins are characteristic

Showy, silvery gray bracts form a ruff around the flowerhead

Minute flowers are grouped into a dense mound

Bees and butterflies find sea hollies very attractive, and on warm, sunny days the flowerheads hum with activity.

SPINE TINGLER
Between midsummer and early autumn *Eryngium × oliverianum* is covered in purple flowerheads. Like all sea hollies, it makes a good flower for arrangements if the stems are cut before the flowers are fully opened.

◄ FLOWER SIZE
2½in (6cm)
across

Lavenders *LAVANDULA*

A HAZE OF PURPLE, the buzzing of bees, and, above all, that wonderful sun-baked fragrance – if anything says "summer" to my senses, it's lavender. Provided there's a dry, sunny spot for them, they suit every garden style imaginable. For an early start to the season, grow traditional English lavenders (*Lavandula angustifolia*) – but be sure to make room, too, for the more unusual French lavender (*L. stoechas*) varieties.

TOUCH OF CLASS
The compact shape and rich color of *Lavandula angustifolia* 'Hidcote' make it perfect for creating a classic English garden edging for a path or border.

IN THE PINK
The subtle, whisper pink of *Lavandula angustifolia* 'Loddon Pink' creates a delicate haze of color and perfume in any sunny spot from mid- to late summer.

THE CLASSIC, *above and right*
In midsummer the mounded, gray-green form of *Lavandula angustifolia* 'Twickel Purple' is brought to life by countless slender purple flower spikes.

GROWING LAVENDERS

PLANT PROFILE

Shrubs; provide winter protection for tender types . *L.angustifolia* and *L. × intermedia* Z 5–8, *L. stoechas* Z 8–9.

- SIZE 10–30in (25–75cm).
- FLOWER COLORS Blue, purple, lilac, pink, white.
- FLOWERING From late spring throughout summer.
- SITE The poorer and drier the soil the better, in full sun.

Soil Lavenders need a very well-drained (preferably alkaline) soil and lots of sun. They thrive on poor soil and need very little feeding.

Pruning Regular trimming in spring is a must to prevent plants from becoming thin and straggly. Combine this with a very light pruning after flowering to remove faded flower spikes, and the plants should remain compact for several years. If grown as hedging, clip into shape in midspring. Even with regular pruning, lavenders usually lose their shape and charm after several years and are best replaced.

Cuttings Take either softwood or semiripe cuttings in late spring or late summer: an easy way to make lots of bedding plants.

Containers In cold areas, grow less hardy lavenders in well-drained containers and move into a frost-free greenhouse or porch over winter.

My favorites *Lavandula angustifolia* 'Twickel Purple'; *L. × intermedia* Dutch Group, *L. × i.* 'Grappenhall'; *L. stoechas, L. s.* f. *leucantha, L. s.* subsp. *pedunculata*. For miniature hedging to edge paths, use *L. angustifolia* 'Hidcote', *L. a.* 'Loddon Pink', or *L. a.* 'Nana Alba'.

CRAZY CHARM, *below*

A lavender that has gone into the dressing room and emerged wearing a chief's headdress, *L. stoechas* has a much zanier appeal than its chic common name of French lavender might suggest. It is more tender than most other lavenders, but if you protect it well it's not difficult to keep over cold winters.

COLOR COORDINATION, *above*

The gray-blue roof and pale blue walls of a nearby house are brought to life by the gray-green foliage and purple flowers of the lavender growing nearby.

Bright pinkish purple featherlike bracts

FLOWERHEAD ▶
2in (5cm)
tall

The tiny flowers are almost overshadowed by the showier bracts

To dry lavender, cut the flower spikes before the flowers are fully open and hang them in bunches upside down in a well-ventilated shed or room.

Nigellas *NIGELLA*

AT THE HEIGHT OF summer, nigellas form a haze of vivid blues and purples, taking the heat out of the flower border. Their delicate flowers and feathery foliage give them a dreamlike quality, but despite their fragile appearance they are one of the easiest annuals to grow from seed, and since they are quite hardy they can be sown direct in spring or the previous autumn. Nigellas make lovely cut flowers. Their drying seedheads add interest to the border for weeks or can be cut and brought indoors for dried flower arrangements.

◄ FLOWER SIZE
1½in (4cm)
across

JEWEL COLORS
Introduce a touch of the exotic with the seed mixture Persian Jewel (*above, right, and opposite*). With pretty blooms in deep violet-blue, sky blue, rose-pink, deep pink, and white, they shine, gemlike, all summer and into autumn.

COTTAGE-GARDEN FAVORITES
Nigellas make attractive gap-fillers in a perennial flower border. Here, they contribute to the cottage-garden feeling, together with foxgloves, peonies, campanulas, and gypsophila.

GROWING NIGELLAS

PLANT PROFILE

Annual: sow seed each year, or allow plants to self-seed at will.

• SIZE 16–20in (40–50cm); dwarf forms 8–10in (20–25cm).

• FLOWER COLORS Blue, purple-lilac, pink, white, yellow.

• FLOWERING Through summer into early autumn; sow in autumn for an early start.

• SITE Ideally, sandy or well-drained soil, in full sun.

Planting Seeds can be sown directly into the flowerbed in autumn or spring, then thinned once the seedlings have appeared. Spring sowings are generally more reliable. Plants usually take 10 to 12 weeks to reach flowering size.

Self-seeding Nigellas spring up everywhere! Move self-sown seedlings, if necessary, as soon as they are large enough to handle in the spring. Flower color may not be exactly the same as last year's plants.

Soil I find that nigellas will tolerate everything but heavy soil.

Dwarf varieties For superb border or path edging, you can't beat the very compact 'Dwarf Moody Blue' or 'Shorty Blue', which reach a height of about 10in (25cm). They are also ideal for containers.

My favorites *Nigella hispanica*; *N. damascena*, *N. d.* 'Miss Jekyll Alba', *N. d.* 'Miss Jekyll Azure Blue', *N. d.* 'Mulberry Rose', *N. d.* 'Oxford Blue', *N. d.* Persian Jewel Series, *N. d.* 'Red Jewel'. I'm intrigued by the seedheads of *N. orientalis* 'Transformer'. Turn them inside out to make silvery buff-colored "flowers" for indoor displays.

To stop nigellas from self-seeding, pick the seedheads as they start to open and gather the seed to sow elsewhere.

Salvias *SALVIA*

THE WARM-CLIMATE ORIGINS of many salvias make them easy to grow on dry, sunny sites, often in situations where other plants would have difficulty surviving. These tall, slender, elegant perennials are quite different from the stocky little red salvias used as bedding plants and the bushy sages grown as cooking herbs, although several have aromatic leaves and all have the same basic flower form and clear, bright flowers. Many need care and a little work to take them through cold winters, but some are quite hardy; for these, winter moisture is a greater enemy than low temperatures.

Individual flowers in tiers create a "cakestand" effect

SEA SPRITE, *left*
Between summer and autumn, the delicate spikes of *Salvia coccinea* 'Coral Nymph' are studded with coral-colored blooms.

DEPTH CHARGE, *right*
Combine the dense, lilac-blue flower spikes of *Salvia × superba* with bright pink poppies for a truly electrifying display.

GROWING SALVIAS

PLANT PROFILE

The salvias described here are perennials; many are tender in most areas.

- SIZE 18–30in (45–75cm).
- FLOWER COLORS Blue, purple, yellow, red, white.
- FLOWERING Early summer to autumn.
- SITE Good drainage is vital, as is lots of sun. For marginally hardy salvias, choose a sheltered spot away from cold winds.

Sowing seeds Perennial salvia species (not the varieties) can be raised from seed, and this is best done by sowing direct into open ground in the spring.

Dividing Established plants can be divided in spring.

Cuttings Where plants are unlikely to survive the winter, take softwood cuttings from late spring to early autumn and then overwinter the young plants in a greenhouse. Harden off before planting out in late spring (after frost) the following year.

Pruning With hardier salvias it is a good idea to remove all the faded flower spikes to stimulate a second flush of flowers at the end of summer or in early autumn. If the less hardy types survive the winter, cut back hard in spring to promote basal branching.

My favorites Hardier types (Z 5–9): *Salvia nemorosa* 'Lubecca', *S. n.* 'Ostfriesland'; *S. × superba*; *S. verticillata* 'Purple Rain'. Less hardy types: *S. coccinea* 'Coral Nymph'; *S. farinacea*, *S. f.* 'Alba', *S. f.* 'Victoria'; *S. greggii*; *S. guaranitica*; 'Indigo Spires; *S. involucrata*; *S. leucantha*; *S. patens*; 'Purple Majesty'.

For a changing display of color, grow Salvia × superba, which has attractive reddish purple bracts that persist on the plant after the lovely flowers have faded.

Although many salvias have pleasantly aromatic foliage, a few, in particular S. sclarea var. turkestanica, emit a distinctly unpleasant smell; sniff before you site them!

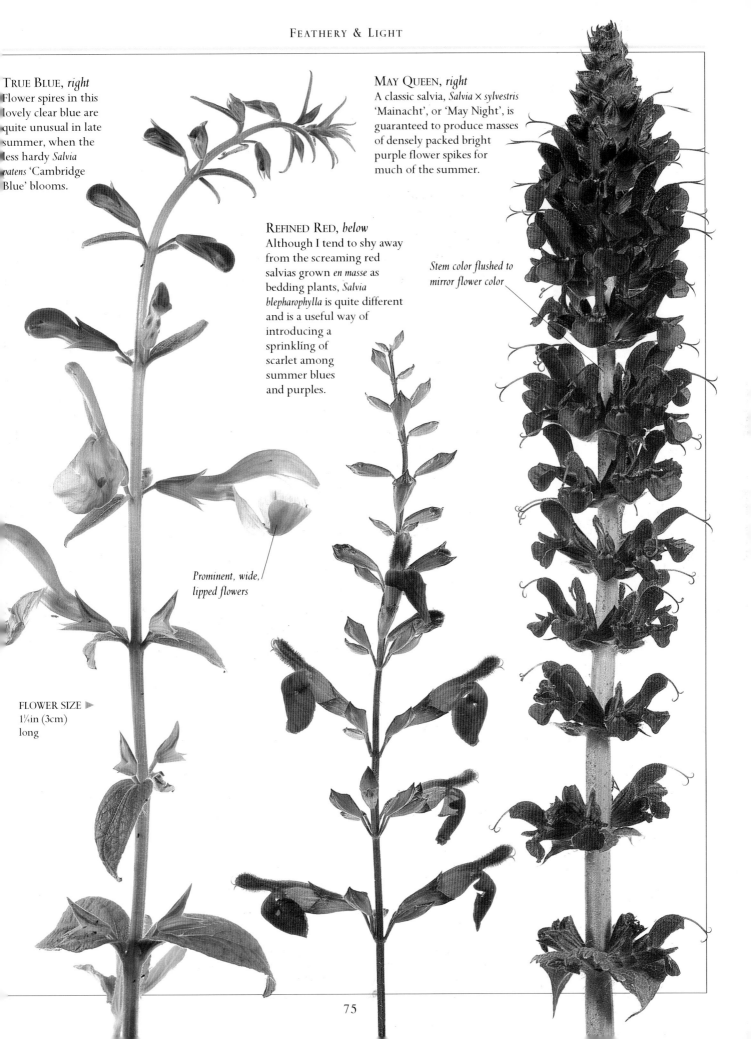

TRUE BLUE, *right*
Flower spires in this lovely clear blue are quite unusual in late summer, when the less hardy *Salvia patens* 'Cambridge Blue' blooms.

MAY QUEEN, *right*
A classic salvia, *Salvia × sylvestris* 'Mainacht', or 'May Night', is guaranteed to produce masses of densely packed bright purple flower spikes for much of the summer.

REFINED RED, *below*
Although I tend to shy away from the screaming red salvias grown *en masse* as bedding plants, *Salvia blepharophylla* is quite different and is a useful way of introducing a sprinkling of scarlet among summer blues and purples.

Stem color flushed to mirror flower color

Prominent, wide, lipped flowers

FLOWER SIZE ▶
1⅛in (3cm) long

Daisy shapes

ASK ALMOST ANYONE TO DRAW AN "INSTANT" PICTURE OF A FLOWER, AND THEY WILL PROBABLY SCRIBBLE DOWN A DAISY SHAPE. SIMPLE, EVEN CHILDISH IN FORM THEY MAY BE, BUT I cannot imagine a garden without some daisylike flowers. I like them for their distinct personalities (think of a radiant sunflower, or of a quirky 'Whirligig' osteospermum) and for their sheer good-natured exuberance – these are the sort of flowers that simply lay themselves open to bask in the sun and reflect their cheer and warmth back on to you! Even better, many of them bring glowing colors as summer ends. Where would we be without rudbeckias, asters, and cosmos as the days start to cool and draw in? As if that were not enough, most of the plants featured in this section also provide great flowers for cutting so that you can enjoy their vibrance indoors, too.

"With their irrepressibly cheerful flowers, sometimes as large as dinner plates . . . sunflowers always lift the spirits."

SUNFLOWERS, PAGES 82—83

Left RUDBECKIAS (PP.88—89), THEIR BRIGHT BLOOMS MAKING A GARDEN SEAT INVITING

Perennial asters ASTER

SUMMER AND AUTUMN WOULDN'T be the same without asters. Their brightly colored flowers, usually with glorious, contrasting golden centers, bring warmth and color into late autumn and give bees and butterflies a reason to linger in the garden. Herbaceous asters, including New England and New York types, are best bought as plants, and, although most often grown in borders, the more compact types also look great in containers or as border or path edging. Given a free-draining soil and plenty of sun, these perennials are easy to grow.

PINK PERFECTION, *left*
You'd probably get away with a pink and yellow outfit only at Ascot, but the semidouble *Aster novi-belgii* 'Little Pink Beauty' carries off its color scheme with style anywhere.

DOUBLE IMPACT
The striking, double, dark pink flowers of *Aster novi-belgii* 'Patricia Ballard' remind me of chimney sweep's brushes atop their sturdy, long stems.

SWEET AND LOW, *above*
From midsummer to midautumn the clump-forming *Aster lateriflorus* 'Horizontalis' produces masses of small white or very pale pink flowers with prominent rose-pink centers.

SPLASH OF COLOR, *left*
Without the pink and purple mounds of color produced by the asters — as exuberant and flamboyant as old-fashioned Sunday hats — this border would be quite subdued.

BLUE DELIGHT
For a less strident-looking aster choose the delicate, lilac-blue spidery flowers of *Aster × frikartii* 'Wunder von Stäfa'. It may need staking or supporting with twiggy sticks.

()

GROWING ASTERS

PLANT PROFILE

Perennials. Z 3–8.

- SIZE 18–60in (45–150cm).
- FLOWER COLORS Blue, purple, lilac, pink, white, usually with contrasting yellow centers.
- FLOWERING Midsummer until late autumn (or until the first frosts).
- SITE Preferably fertile and well-drained, alkaline or slightly acidic soil, in full sun.

Dividing Divide every three or four years in early spring.

Sowing seeds Only the species asters can be raised from seed. Seeds sown in spring often result in flowering plants the same autumn.

Plant problems To minimize the risk of powdery mildew to which asters are prone, keep plants moist at the roots by adequate watering toward the end of summer and in early autumn. Mulching also helps, as does ensuring good air circulation by making sure plants are not crowded.

My favorites Aster amellus 'King George'; A. divaricatus; A. ericoides 'Pink Cloud'; A. × frikartii 'Mönch', A. × f. 'Wunder von Stäfa'; A. lateriflorus 'Horizontalis'; A. novae-angliae 'Andenken an Alma Potschke', A. n-a. 'Harrington's Pink', A. n-a. 'Purple Dome', A. n-a. 'Septemberrubin'; A. novi-belgii 'Patricia Ballard', A. n-b. 'Winston S. Churchill'; A. tataricus.

The lovely Aster × frikartii 'Mönch' (here planted with rudbeckias) is one of the most mildew-resistant of asters.

FUNGUS FREE
Many asters are vulnerable to the dreaded powdery mildew disease; to avoid this, grow Aster amellus 'Blue King' or other A. amellus varieties, which have good resistance.

FLOWER SIZE ▶
1¼–2in (3–5cm) across

Marguerites *ARGYRANTHEMUM*

GIVEN THE CHOICE between marguerites and their relatives the chrysanthemums, I'd go for the former every time. Whether you grow them in beds, borders, or containers, with well-drained soil and plenty of sun they can be guaranteed to produce masses of wide-eyed, innocent, daisylike flowers throughout the summer and often into autumn. Sadly, although they will withstand winters in a Mediterranean climate, they are not hardy in colder regions and are usually treated as unreliably hardy perennials or as annuals. Nevertheless, their flowers are so reliable and so pretty, and their flowering period so long, that they are worth the effort of overwintering or raising them from cuttings each year.

GROWING MARGUERITES

PLANT PROFILE

Woody-based perennials often grown as annuals. Z 10–11.

- SIZE 12–20in (30–50cm).
- FLOWER COLORS Yellow, pink, white.
- FLOWERING Throughout summer and into autumn.
- SITE Well-drained soil or soil mix and full sun are essential if you are to get the best possible display of flowers. Keep top-heavy standards away from strong winds.

Planting Plant out only after any danger of frost is over. If necessary, improve drainage first, using coarse sand and organic matter.

Cuttings Semiripe cuttings, 2–4in (5–10cm), are best taken in late summer and then overwintered in a cool but frost-free greenhouse. You can also take softwood cuttings in spring. Always choose healthy, nonflowering shoots.

Pruning No need to prune, but pinching out shoot tips forms well-branched, bushy young plants.

Deadheading Regularly picking off dead flowers extends the flowering period, so deadhead as soon as any flowers fade.

Plant problems Leaf miners may will attack foliage, but although the pale wiggly lines they produce may look unsightly, they do little harm to the plants.

My favorites 'Chelsea Girl' (white with yellow centers), 'Jamaica Primrose' (warm yellow), 'Snowflake' (pure white, semi-double), 'Vancouver' (deep pink with a prominent pink center).

In sheltered spots in mild areas, you may be able to overwinter plants provided the soil never gets too wet and the crowns are mulched with a deep layer of pine needles, loose leaves, or straw.

For real impact, especially for a container, invest in a marguerite that has been trained as a standard.

FLOWER POWER, *below*
Throughout summer and often until early autumn, or sometimes until first frosts, *Argyranthemum frutescens* is a mass of pretty white flowers.

◀ FLOWER SIZE
¾in (2cm) across

'lim yet sturdy
ark green stems
old flowers erect

Petals often curve back slightly and are marked with distinct ridges

CONTAINED JOY, *above*
Their compact, upright habit makes marguerites perfect for containers. Here, they are combined prettily with petunias; deadhead both plants regularly.

STAR ATTRACTION, *right*
These open, daisylike flowers – here, 'Apricot Sunrise' – are a magnet for many insects, including bees and hoverflies, whose larvae are ravenous aphid-eaters.

CENTER OF ATTENTION
Some marguerites have large, elaborate "anemone" centers. The vigorous 'Vancouver' has double, deep pink flowers fading to buff-pink with age.

CARIBBEAN CHARMER
The petals of 'Jamaica Primrose' are the color of their spring-flowering namesake, but the golden center of each flower adds a more exotic touch.

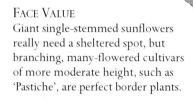

Sunflowers *HELIANTHUS*

WITH THEIR IRREPRESSIBLY cheerful flowers sometimes as large as dinner plates and their phenomenal rate of growth, sunflowers always lift the spirits. Easy to grow in sun or part shade, traditionally they were flowers for children to raise in a corner of the kitchen garden – but today, they appear in the most sophisticated flower arrangements.

One happy result is a growing choice of varieties for gardeners, in shades of yellow, red, buff, or brown, often dusted with pinks and bronzes.

FACE VALUE
Giant single-stemmed sunflowers really need a sheltered spot, but branching, many-flowered cultivars of more moderate height, such as 'Pastiche', are perfect border plants.

MIXED BAG
One of the smaller sunflowers, 'Music Box Mixed' bears large numbers of very variably colored, dark-centered flowers.

A HEAD START
For the impact of large flowers without the gigantic height that you would expect, 'Sunspot' is an excellent choice.

TARGET PRACTICE
The radiating blushes of color on newer cultivars such as 'Pastiche' accentuate the giant central "landing pads" for bees.

GROWING SUNFLOWERS

PLANT PROFILE
The plants described here are all annuals – *Helianthus annuus*.

• SIZE 30in–10ft (75cm–3m).

• FLOWER COLORS Yellows from lemon to gold; pink, red, buff, cream, brown.

• FLOWERING Throughout summer and into autumn.

• SITE Sunflowers will grow in almost any soil, but for best results choose a heavy loam in full sun or part shade.

Sowing seeds Growing sunflowers couldn't be simpler. Just clear the soil and sow the seeds direct, about ½in (1cm) deep, in spring. Since their flowers will always face the sun, make sure that you plant them in a position where you, and not the neighbors, will be able to enjoy them!

Plant care Young plants must be watered regularly, but once growing strongly, sunflowers need very little attention. It is worth keeping them protected from the ravages of slugs when the plants are young.

Support If your garden is windy, you will either need to stake your sunflowers or choose 'Incredible' or 'Music Box', which are low-growing varieties.

For cutting Sunflowers make superb cut flowers; I always grow enough to bring some into the house. Cut them when they are coming into color, then allow them to open out while in the vase, providing them with a cut-flower food. Some varieties will last for two to three weeks in water.

My favorites 'Giant Single', 'Incredible', 'Italian White', 'Moonwalker', 'Music Box', 'Sunbeam', 'Sunspot', 'Taiyo', 'Teddy Bear', 'Velvet Queen'. For cut flowers, I choose branching cultivars of medium height, such as 'Pastiche', 'Prado Red', 'Prado Yellow', 'Valentine', and 'Toybox'.

SUN KING
The towering stems of 'Giant Single'
are topped with huge flowers in a
gorgeous, rich lemon yellow, their
velvety russet-brown centers dusted
with golden pollen.

◄ FLOWER SIZE
10in (25cm)
across

*Kaleidoscopic
golds and browns
in the center*

*Smaller flowers
develop on short
sideshoots*

*Ripe sunflower seeds are easily
removed to keep for spring
sowing or for feeding the birds
during the winter months.*

Cosmos *COSMOS*

THE DAISY-SHAPED flowers, long slender stems, and fine, fernlike foliage of cosmos add up, quite simply, to perfection – the flowers are so faultless they look as if punched from plastic! Both the annuals and perennials are generally easy to grow; they thrive in sunny, well-drained sites, even on the poorest soils, so are useful for creating splashes of color where other plants would fail. The annuals can be raised from seed and will flower profusely from midsummer onward.

CHOCAHOLIC HEAVEN
Whether viewed *en masse* (*left*) or close up (*right*), the flowers of *Cosmos atrosanguineus* are truly sumptuous, and a quick sniff proves that the flowers really do smell of top-quality chocolate.

◄ FLOWER SIZE
1¾in (4.5cm) across

GROWING COSMOS

PLANT PROFILE
Annuals and perennials.
Cosmos atrosanguineus Z 7–10.
- SIZE 2–3ft (60–90cm).
- FLOWER COLORS Red, orange, yellow, pink, white, brown.
- FLOWERING Throughout the summer until autumn, or the first frosts.
- SITE Best in a poor, sandy soil, in full sun; will perform quite well in semi-shade.

Sowing seeds Annuals and some species can be sown from seed. Sow at 61°F (16°C) in early spring, then harden off and plant out in late spring, or sow *in situ* in late spring. Many of them are best left to reseed.

Cuttings *Cosmos atrosanguineus* and other perennials can be grown from root cuttings in a propagating case in early spring, or from basal stem cuttings taken in spring.

Fantastic flowers Regular deadheading ensures the largest flower size and longest possible flowering period.

Staking It is often necessary to stake taller cosmos, especially if grown on richer soil.

Feeding Cosmos thrive in poor conditions, so avoid feeding; this may make them leggy and can even delay flowering.

My favorites *Cosmos bipinnatus* 'Daydream', *C. b.* 'Picotee', *C. b.* 'Sea Shells', *C. b.* 'Sensation'; *C. sulfureus* 'Bright Lights', *C. s.* Klondyke Series, *C. s.* Ladybird Series. *C. atrosanguineus* will bring delicious chocolate aromas into your garden. For exposed sites, dwarf *C. bipinnatus* 'Sonata' is ideal.

Grow cosmos in pots to brighten up terraces, patios, and garden steps.

Cosmos make good cut flowers, so it's worth growing a few specifically for this purpose. The taller varieties are best for flower arranging, since their longer stems make them easier to display in a vase or combine with other flowers.

FLOWER SIZE ▶
3in (7.5cm)
across

SEASIDE TREAT, *above*
The elaborate petals of the annual
Cosmos bipinnatus 'Sea Shells' bring a
dizzy splash of color whether grown
in containers or in a border.

BEAUTY QUEEN, *right*
The name cosmos comes
from the Greek *kosmos*,
meaning beautiful. Most
cosmos are good for
cutting – I like to bring
some indoors so that I can
take a closer look at the
lovely and intriguing
details of each bloom.

SUMMER SPIN, *left*
Plant different varieties of *Cosmos
bipinnatus* in drifts for flowers
produced in profusion for much of
the summer, complete with a
backdrop of fine, ferny foliage.

85

Osteospermums Osteospermu

THE DIZZY PRETTINESS OF osteospermums is well worth the bit of extra effort that their tenderness demands in many areas. Provided they have plenty of sun and a dry or free-draining soil, they will be covered in cheerful, daisylike flowers throughout the summer months. Whether they are grown in containers or in a border, their striking, slightly clownish looks and crazy petal shapes are guaranteed to bring a smile to your face.

The center reminds me of a honeycomb, with orange and brown bees clustered around it

WHITE WHIRL, *right*
'Whirligig White' has an intriguing lilac flush to the petals and center.

◀ FLOWER SIZE
2in (5cm)
across

PINK SENSATION, *above*
The vibrant pink flowers of 'Stardust' burst out like stars in sunshine.

BUTTERY SPREAD, *right*
Delicate creamy yellow 'Buttermilk' has a serene presence in the border.

OUT OF AFRICA, *above*
The dark center of 'African Summer' contrasts with its gray-white petals.

WHIZ KID, *right*
The startling outline of 'Whirligig Pink' is created by the pinched petal ends.

GROWING OSTEOSPERMUMS

PLANT PROFILE

Annuals or marginally hardy perennials; bring plants into a protected spot over winter. Z 10–11.

- SIZE 12–24in (30–60cm).
- FLOWER COLORS Yellow, blue, purple, lilac, pink, white, cream.
- FLOWERING Throughout summer.
- SITE Free-draining soil, in full sun.

Planting Named varieties should be available for sale as plants in spring and summer. Because osteospermums tend to flop, grow in groups, stake loosely, or plant close to other plants with a more attractive shape.

Soil A well-drained soil is essential. On heavier soils, plants are likely to grow poorly or die, even in mild weather. Incorporate plenty of sand in all but the most free-draining soils.

Sowing seeds Species can be raised from seed sown in late winter to early spring for flowering the

following summer. Sow them under glass and plant out after the last frosts. Propagate named varieties from semiripe cuttings taken toward the end of summer and then rooted in a sandy soil mix in a greenhouse.

Protection If you can't bring them under glass, they may survive frost with a deep mulch of straw, bark chips, or leaves, but drainage must also be good.

My favorites 'Blackthorn Seedling', 'Buttermilk', 'Cannington John', 'Pink Whirls', 'Silver Sparkler', 'Stardust', 'Whirligig'.

When grown next to a gravel path, osteospermums form excellent edging, and the gravel helps provide good drainage.

Rudbeckias *RUDBECKIA*

THE BOLD DAISY shapes and rich flower colors of rudbeckias (including the gloriosa daisies) have an enduring appeal. In various shades of orange, yellow, and brown, they bring a golden warmth to any border from summer right until early autumn. They are very easy to grow, and although they prefer a fairly moist soil and plenty of sun, they still flower reasonably well even in light shade. In shadier conditions they tend to get very tall, and if sunlight is in really short supply they may flop over, but the flowers will still keep coming. Named perennial varieties are best bought as young plants, but species and annuals can be raised from seed.

FOREVER GOLD, *above*
From late summer until well into midautumn, *Rudbeckia fulgida* var. *speciosa* 'Viette's Little Suzy' is a mass of golden daisy flowers set against midgreen leaves.

SHORT BUT SWEET, *right*
Usually grown as an annual, the low-growing *Rudbeckia hirta* 'Becky Mixed' produces a fine display in golds and browns.

SIGNS OF AUTUMN, *left*
Like warm autumn sunshine, the bright yellow flowers and green-yellow centers of 'Herbstsonne' glow from midsummer to early autumn. As they age the centers turn brown, a reminder that darker days are to follow.

GROWING RUDBECKIAS

PLANT PROFILE

Annuals and perennials. Z 3–9.

• SIZE Most 24–40in (60–100cm); *Rudbeckia laciniata* and its varieties can grow to 6ft (1.8m).

• FLOWER COLORS Orange, yellow, brown.

• FLOWERING Throughout summer and into early autumn.

• SITE Fairly moist soil, with plenty of sun, although they will tolerate light shade.

Planting It is possible to grow rudbeckias in soil that tends to become dry, but if they are to thrive you should incorporate plenty of coarse organic matter into the soil at planting and regularly mulch and water them.

Invasiveness Watch out for *Rudbeckia laciniata* 'Hortensia' on fertile soils; it may become invasive.

Sowing seeds Sow seeds of annuals in early spring in a propagating case. Harden off, then plant out in late spring.

Dividing Established perennials can be divided in either spring or autumn. Autumn may be preferable, since the soil tends to remain moist, giving newly divided plants plenty of time to establish themselves before the onset of drying summer weather.

My favorites *Rudbeckia fulgida* var. *speciosa* 'Viette's Little Suzy', *R. f.* var. *sullivantii* 'Goldsturm'; 'Herbstsonne' (also known as 'Autumn Sun'); *R. hirta* 'Goldilocks', *R. h.* 'Irish Eyes', *R. h.* 'Marmalade'; *R. laciniata* 'Goldquelle'; *R. maxima*.

CROWD PLEASER
Rudbeckias make a cheerful contribution to any mixed planting, but for a really exuberant effect, try them alone in great masses, as here, crowding a garden bench – a really inviting place to sit!

POT OF GOLD
The flowers of *Rudbeckia fulgida* var. *sullivantii*
'Goldsturm' are larger than most and a
rich, glowing yellow-orange. It grows to
about knee-high, and from a distance its
flowers look like mounds of gold coins.

◀ FLOWER SIZE
up to 4½in (12cm)
across

*The taller rudbeckias, and those
grown in a shaded position, often
need staking, so to avoid this,
grow varieties under 3ft (90cm)
in height and choose a
sunny spot.*

*Rudbeckias make great, long-
lasting cut flowers for late
summer and autumn.*

*Once the first flowering of
Rudbeckia hirta is over, cut
them back hard and feed with
liquid fertilizer to encourage a
second flush of flowers.*

Trumpets & bells

WE MAY NOT BE ABLE TO HEAR THE MUSIC THEY MAKE, BUT WHEREVER YOU SEE FLOWERS SHAPED LIKE TRUMPETS AND BELLS, YOU'LL HEAR THE BUZZING OF BEES, HUMMING AWAY TO THE sound of some silent symphony. Even the flowers themselves seem to be nodding and swaying along – it takes only a breath of wind to set them bobbing, bringing movement and life into the garden, as fascinating to watch as their busy visitors. The flowers here all share this animated elegance, but, like the musical instruments they mimic, they vary considerably in tone. If dainty fritillaries and dicentras really belong to the players in some fairy orchestra, then bolder trumpets such as daffodils, and those where several flowers are grouped together on single stems, such as agapanthus, look to me like a pretty powerful loudspeaker system!

"Late spring sees the arrival of fritillaries, their delicate flowers nodding in the slightest breeze."

FRITILLARIES, PAGES 100—101

Left CAMPANULAS (PP.96—97) BRING A REFRESHING BREATH OF THE MEADOW TO THE BORDER

Agapanthus *AGAPANTHUS*

THE NAME AGAPANTHUS comes from the Greek for "love flower," and I can't think of a more apt derivation for these beautiful blooms. They bring back happy memories of my travels to Madeira and South Africa, where they can be seen growing in huge numbers – an unforgettable sight. Agapanthus are available as plants (it takes several years for plants grown from seed to reach flowering size), and provided they are supplied with a moist, fertile soil and plenty of sun, they are fairly easy to grow. They have a long flowering season, from midsummer to early autumn, and most flower reliably for many years.

FIRM FAVORITES, *left*
One of the more widely grown agapanthus are the Headbourne Hybrids, which are also among the most reliably hardy.

GROWING AGAPANTHUS

PLANT PROFILE

Perennials; winter protection is necessary in many areas. Z 7–10.

- SIZE Most 2–3ft (60–90cm), but some may reach 44in (110cm).
- FLOWER COLORS Blue, purple, lilac, white.
- FLOWERING Midsummer to early autumn.
- SITE Rich, moist soil, in full sun, sheltered from wind.

Planting Plant crowns 2in (5cm) below the soil surface in midspring.

Dividing Divide and replant in mid- to late spring. They don't like being disturbed, so try to keep clumps in one place and divide only when they are really congested.

Pruning Cut back flowerheads once flowering is over, unless you are saving them for drying or a winter arrangement.

Frost protection A mulch, 4–6in (10–15cm) deep, is usually adequate. A free-draining material that remains relatively dry, such as pine needles or straw, is preferable to something that retains moisture around the crown. If necessary, hold the mulch in position using a covering of chicken wire. Plunge pots and containers or wrap them in a jacket of burlap, bubble wrap, or similar material.

My favorites 'Blue Giant', 'Bressingham Blue', 'Bressingham Bounty', 'Bressingham White', *Agapanthus campanulatus* 'Isis', Headbourne Hybrids, 'Lilliput'.

GRAND DESIGN, *left*
With magnificent flowerheads like these, it is no wonder that agapanthus make fabulous cut flowers.

HIDDEN CHARMS
In contrast to more showy agapanthus, the discreet charm of *Agapanthus inapertus* lies in its drooping, languorous, dark purple flowers.

Individual
trumpet-shaped
blooms

◀ FLOWERHEAD
4in (10cm)
across

SUMMER SNOWFALL
When in full bloom in late summer, the bell-shaped white flowerheads of 'Snowy Owl' resemble a mass of starry ice crystals, bringing a cool note to a late season border.

Agapanthus make elegant and unusual edging for a wide path, particularly one adjacent to a fence or wall, where their generous height will not dwarf neighboring plants.

Provided they are kept moist, try growing agapanthus in large containers; they look great grown in pots with a hint of blue in the glaze.

BOLD BEDFELLOWS, *right*
Agapanthus are no retiring wallflowers, and they need strong forms and colors from their companion plants to set them off. Here, planted with yellow-green *Cortaderia selloana* 'Aureolineata', a golden arborvitae, and boisterous pinkish red penstemons, the agapanthus 'Loch Hope' makes a particularly striking display.

Columbines *Aquilegia*

THE COMMON NAME OF these pretty perennials comes from the Latin *columbinus* – meaning dovelike – and the gentle flowers do indeed remind me of groups of doves, billing and cooing. Their fairytale quality is reinforced by delicate, almost feathery foliage – similar to that of the lovely maidenhair fern – for which alone they merit space in a border. Columbines are often quite short-lived, so expect to replace them every few years or as soon as they start to lose vigor. They like a moist, well-drained soil and will grow in sun or part shade.

◀ FLOWER SIZE
3¼in (8cm) long

REAR VIEW, *above*
The curving spurs behind columbine flowers are very well developed on some varieties, as with this bright 'Crimson Star'.

SHADY PAIR, *right*
The pale flowers of *Aquilegia vulgaris,* combined with *Meconopsis cambrica* (Welsh poppies), bring a light touch to a shady corner of the garden.

PICK OF THE BUNCH
Among the taller columbines, the McKana hybrids are deservedly popular for their wide range of flower colors.

HAT TRICK
Aquilegia vulgaris and its varieties – here 'Adelaide Addison' – are known as "Granny's bonnets."

ICE MAIDEN, *right*
The cool, translucent beauty of 'Dorothy' looks its best in a shady spot.

GROWING COLUMBINES

PLANT PROFILE
Perennials, although they are often short-lived. Z 3–9.
- SIZE 12–36in (30–90cm).
- FLOWER COLORS Red, yellow, blue, purple, lilac, pink, white, cream.
- FLOWERING Late spring to midsummer.
- SITE Moist but well-drained soil; they will grow in full sun, but part shade suits them best.

Sowing seeds In early spring in a cold frame, or outdoors in summer. Don't transplant young seed-raised plants until the autumn.

Planting Add some leafmold to the soil when planting and you will be rewarded with plants that establish quickly and flower really well.

Dividing Established clumps of columbines can be divided in autumn or early spring.

Pruning Cut back flower stems after flowering if self-seeded plants become a nuisance.

Self-seeding Columbines self-seed readily and usually reestablish very well when transplanted, so gather seedlings and young plants from around the bases of their parents and use them to fill gaps elsewhere. Interesting "new" flower color combinations may develop from these seedlings, since they will not be the same as the parent plant.

My favorites *Aquilegia caerulea; A. canadensis, A. c.* 'Nana'; 'Crimson Star'; 'Dorothy'; *A. formosa; A. fragrans; A. longissima;* 'Magpie'; McKana Group; 'Snow Queen'; *A. vulgaris, A. v.* 'Adelaide Addison', *A. v.* 'Nivea'.

The smaller alpine species and varieties are exquisite additions to rock gardens and troughs.

Campanulas *CAMPANULA*

ALL CAMPANULAS HAVE a lovely, relaxed, cottage-garden feeling to them, and, good-natured as they are, they will grow in most conditions. Some are a bit too eager — *Campanula portenschlagiana* and *C. poscharskyana* are very invasive and will need to be clipped back regularly if you don't want them to swamp everything in sight. Campanulas are sometimes known as bellflowers (or "little bells," as the Latin name suggests). With some, the pointed petals curve back to form curled lips; in others, they open wide, making tiny stars.

GROWING CAMPANULAS

PLANT PROFILE

Most are perennials. Z 3–9.

- SIZE The range is huge, from low-growing forms just a few inches high to a statuesque 5ft (1.5m).
- FLOWER COLORS Purple, blue, lilac, pink, white.
- FLOWERING Spring into summer.
- SITE They prefer a fairly well-drained soil, in sun or part shade.

Propagation Sow seed in mid-autumn or early to midspring in a cold frame or cold greenhouse. Pot on, then plant out one year later. Divide mature plants in autumn or spring.

Support Stake tall forms with twiggy sticks early in the season. In exposed gardens, grow shorter varieties to avoid needing to stake.

Flower care Deadhead regularly to encourage further flowering.

My favorites *Campanula alliariifolia*; *C. americana*; *C. carpatica* 'Blue Clips', *C. c.* 'Bressingham White'; *C. glomerata* 'Superba'; *C. lactiflora* 'Loddon Anna', *C. l.* 'Prichard's Variety', *C. l.* 'White Pouffe'; *C. latifolia* 'Gloaming'; *C. persicifolia, C. p.* 'Chettle Charm'; *C. poscharskyana; C. takesimana.*

FLOWER SIZE ▶
2¼in (5.5cm) long

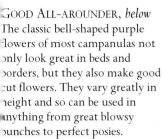

GOOD ALL-AROUNDER, *below*
The classic bell-shaped purple
flowers of most campanulas not
only look great in beds and
borders, but they also make good
cut flowers. They vary greatly in
height and so can be used in
anything from great blowsy
bunches to perfect posies.

*Flowers are
visited by
bees regularly*

COUNTRY LASS
The elegant, pendulous pink and
white bells of 'Elizabeth' are
unlike those of most other
campanulas and bring a
delicate touch to a cottage
garden.

SUMMER MADNESS
Whether you like them or not,
the near-spherical purple-violet
globes produced by *Campanula
glomerata* 'Superba' certainly
create great impact in their own
rather eccentric style.

PEACHY BEAUTY
The medium-sized *Campanula
persicifolia* is sometimes known as
the peach-leaved bellflower. It
looks marvelous held above
clumps of pale pink *Geranium* ×
oxonianum 'Wargrave Pink'.

*Low-growing campanulas such
as this* Campanula
portenschlagiana *can be
allowed to fill gaps between
paving or in walls, where they
won't smother other plants.*

SIMPLY WILD, *right*
Planted randomly,
Campanula persicifolia
helps add color and
simple prettiness to
a planting
accentuating a
waterfall.

Bleeding hearts *DICENTRA*

FROM THE MOMENT they appear above the ground in spring to the time they die back in summer or autumn, bleeding hearts are a handsome addition to the garden. Their foliage, often feathery and fernlike, sometimes much divided, comes in many shades, from bright apple green to soft grayish blue. The flowers are a knockout, dripping like jewels from poised, arching stems and, close up, exquisitely formed, from the tiny lockets of *Dicentra formosa* to the bolder bleeding hearts of *D. spectabilis*. These perennials like a damp but well-drained soil, but apart from that will tolerate a range of growing conditions, from full sun to part shade. Although they may appear miserable in deep shade, they are more adaptable than one is often led to believe.

TRUE HEARTS
The unusually shaped pink and white flowers of *Dicentra spectabilis* look like miniature bleeding hearts clustered along the flower stem. They grace the border in spring and early summer.

GROWING BLEEDING HEARTS

PLANT PROFILE

Perennials. Z 3–9.

• SIZE 12–30in (30–75cm).

• FLOWER COLORS Red, yellow, pink, white, cream.

• FLOWERING From mid-spring into early autumn.

• SITE Prefer moist conditions in well-drained soil. Will grow in sun and part shade and may even perform in deep shade. *D. spectabilis* dies down in summer; fill in the site with annuals.

Planting Add leafmold or well-rotted compost at planting to help encourage soil moisture retention.

Dividing You can divide well-established clumps between autumn and early winter, but try to avoid too much damage to the fragile crown, or divisions are likely to fail. Discard old, woody parts.

Cuttings Take 3–4in (7.5–10cm) root cuttings (see p.41) in spring.

Place them in sandy soil mix or cuttings medium in a cold frame. Grow them on and plant out the following spring. This is the best way to propagate the fragile-rooted *Dicentra spectabilis* without disturbing it.

Sowing seeds Sow seed in spring at 59°F (15°C) and plant out in autumn, or in early spring the following year on heavier soils.

Self-seeding The hybrids self-seed readily, so if you don't mind growing specimens that bear variable resemblance to their parents, they are well worth keeping.

Planting associations The ferny foliage of any bleeding heart looks lovely in a slightly shaded spot among groups of hardy ferns.

My favorites 'Adrian Bloom'; 'Bacchanal'; 'Bountiful'; *Dicentra cucullaria*; *D. eximia*; *D. formosa*; 'Langtrees'; 'Luxuriant'; 'Snowflakes'; *D. spectabilis*, *D. s.* 'Alba'; 'Stuart Boothman'. Plant the climbing *D. scandens* so that it can scramble through a shrub, ornamenting it with its yellow and white flowers.

Individual blooms move gently in the breeze

Dainty flowers are surprisingly weather-resistant

AMAZING GRACE, *right*
The supremely elegant *Dicentra spectabilis* 'Alba' has long arching flower stems decked with the purest white flowers, so waxy and perfect that they seem almost unreal.

CRIMSON SHADES
'Bacchanal' is ideal for naturalizing under shrubs, where it will form attractive spreading clumps with dusky crimson flowers from mid- to late spring.

SPRING ROMANCE, *above*
With its pretty pendent flowers and delicate bluish green divided foliage, *Dicentra spectabilis* makes a handsome addition to an informal border in spring and early summer.

Dicentra spectabilis starts to flower early, so bear this in mind when planning. Choose a site sheltered from any spring frosts or strong winds to avoid damage to young growth.

Dicentras don't like being moved because they have small, fragile roots that fracture readily, so disturb them only when necessary.

◄ FLOWER SIZE
1in (2.5cm)
across

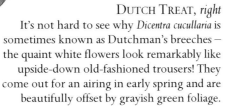

DUTCH TREAT, *right*
It's not hard to see why *Dicentra cucullaria* is sometimes known as Dutchman's breeches — the quaint white flowers look remarkably like upside-down old-fashioned trousers! They come out for an airing in early spring and are beautifully offset by grayish green foliage.

Fritillaries *Fritillaria*

LATE SPRING SEES the arrival of fritillaries, their delicate flowers nodding in the slightest breeze. The first time I saw wild fritillaries was in an alpine meadow in Austria, their dainty heads almost hidden among the grass. It is easy to re-create this effect in the garden, with bulbs planted in miniature drifts or allowed to naturalize in grass. Use them to enhance a grassy bank or, if shade-tolerant, as unusual underplanting below trees. Fritillaries also make a wonderful display in pots or raised beds, where their flowers are brought closer to the eye for inspection – use very sandy soil mix in containers.

Lantern-shaped flowers are ornately patterned

CHECKERED BEAUTY
Often known as snakeshead fritillary, *Fritillaria meleagris* has subtly checkered flowers. It is one of the most widely available fritillaries.

◀ FLOWER SIZE
1¾in (4.5cm) long

Long, slender stems support the nodding flowers

IN THE SHADE
Clusters of green-cream flowers are borne by *Fritillaria pallidiflora*, an excellent choice for lightening up a dull corner.

DEEP AND DUSKY
Bring a touch of glamour to the border with the regal, elegant flowers of *Fritillaria camschatcensis*, in rich, deep purple.

BELLS FOR SPRING
The bell-shaped flowers of *Fritillaria acmopetala* hang on drooping stems where they nod with the slightest breeze.

GROWING FRITILLARIES

PLANT PROFILE
Bulbs that flower each year. Z 3–9.
- SIZE Most 10–18in (25-45cm); *Fritillaria imperialis* and *F. persica* may reach 3ft (90cm).
- FLOWER COLORS Red, orange, yellow, purple/lilac, pink, white, cream, brown.
- FLOWERING Mid- to late spring.
- SITE Free-draining but moist soil in sun or part shade.

Planting Planting depths will vary depending on bulb size, but 4in (10cm) is average. The bulbs do not store well, so buy them as soon as they become available and plant right away. They dislike too moist a soil, particularly once flowering is over, so incorporate plenty of sand at planting. Try growing them toward the edges of shrubs so that they can benefit from the protection that the shrub provides, but not so close that they will be swamped by it.

Dividing If clumps become very congested, lift and separate offsets in autumn.

Firm fixtures Fritillaries don't like being moved, so if they are being swamped by a nearby shrub, it is better to prune the shrub (if you can) than risk moving them. If you must move them, do so when the foliage has died back, and try to take plenty of soil, too.

Naturalizing Gently scatter the bulbs over the grass and plant them where they fall to produce a random, natural look. After flowering, it is important to allow the foliage to die back naturally before attempting to mow the grass (usually several weeks).

My favorites *Fritillaria affinis*; *F. camschatcensis*; *F. involucrata*; *F. meleagris alba*; *F. messanensis*, *F. m.* subsp. *gracilis*; *F. michailovskyi*; *F. pallidiflora*; *F. persica*; *F. pontica*; *F. pyrenaica*. *F. uva-vulpis* is excellent for naturalizing in damp soil; choose *F. meleagris* in drier areas. Try growing *F. meleagris* below deciduous shrubs such as barberries or viburnums, or add them to a carpet of other bulbs and wildflowers. They also look stunning combined with small yellow tulips or *Anemone nemorosa* and *A. blanda*. I've grown them successfully in pots using sandy soil mix under "permanent" plants such as shrubs.

Central cluster of chunky stamens

Petals have an unusual waxy sheen

FLOWER SIZE ▶
1¼in (3cm)
long

MEADOW SWEET
Is there a more lovely sight in
spring than natural drifts of
fritillaries growing in rough
grass? As with any meadow-style
planting, you must leave the
grass uncut so that the leaves
can nourish the bulbs before
dying down.

Leaves are sturdy and spear-shaped

RARE CHARMER
Still showing slight checkering, the brownish
purple, waxy flowers of *Fritillaria michailovskyi* have
a contrasting yellow rim. Very different from
the shyer but hardier snakeshead fritillaries,
they need protection in very cold winters.

*When naturalizing bulbs in a
small area, you can use a bulb
planter, but it is often easier to
lift pieces of sod carefully,
loosen the soil, add fertilizer,
and then plant the bulbs about
4in (10cm) deep before
replacing the sod and watering
in well. Make sure that you
scatter the bulbs to create a
random pattern — no neat lines!*

Nicotianas *NICOTIANA*

BEING A PARTICULAR FAN of scented flowers, I take special delight in those varieties of nicotiana that emit their pervasive fragrance as dusk falls and color drains from the garden. These annuals are some of the easiest flowers to grow, and they are well suited to life in a border or in a container. They perform equally well in sun or part shade, usually flowering solidly throughout summer and into the autumn. The plants are sturdy and very tolerant of most weather extremes; they soon recover if set back by cold or battered by rain.

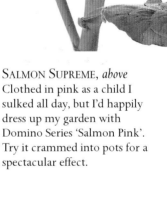

SALMON SUPREME, *above*
Clothed in pink as a child I sulked all day, but I'd happily dress up my garden with Domino Series 'Salmon Pink'. Try it crammed into pots for a spectacular effect.

FRAGRANT FANFARE, *left*
The elegant *Nicotiana alata* has long, trumpet-shaped flowers held on long stems, but it is their perfume that is their real charm.

GROWING NICOTIANAS

PLANT PROFILE

Grown as annuals.

- SIZE Most 10–14in (25–35cm); *Nicotiana alata* and *N. sylvestris* grow to 5ft (1.5m).
- FLOWER COLORS Red, yellow, green, pink, white, cream.
- FLOWERING Throughout the summer.
- SITE Prefer moist, fertile soil, but grow almost anywhere, in full sun or part shade.

Sowing seeds With a greenhouse or propagating case it's very easy to grow nicotianas from seed. Sow in early spring and plant out in late spring, after any danger of late frosts.

Containers Barrels, pots, and windowboxes look wonderful crammed full of nicotianas, and if you choose the scented ones for containers near open windows, you can enjoy their perfume inside, too.

Growing tip The stems and leaves of these plants usually have an unpleasant, almost sticky texture, which is perfectly natural.

Hardiness Where marginally hardy, it may be possible to overwinter plants if you cut them back and cover them with a deep, loose mulch before the first autumn frosts, but this is not always reliable and not really worthwhile when raising new plants is so easy.

My favorites *Nicotiana alata* 'Grandiflora', Domino Series 'Salmon Pink', 'Fragrant Cloud', 'Havana' mix, 'Havana Appleblossom', *N. langsdorffii*, 'Lime Green'. For strong perfume, try *N. alata*, Domino Mixed, Sensation Mixed, *N. sylvestris*, or the dwarf 'White Bedder'.

Generally, nicotianas are best grown in groups or drifts, but the tall Nicotiana sylvestris, *which forms fragrant candelabras of pure white flowers, makes so much impact that it works well grown singly among other flowers in a border. The flowers close up in hot sunshine but open again to release their heady scent in the evening.*

LEMON AND LIME
Like so many other annuals, nicotianas make excellent gap fillers among other plants. Here, *Nicotiana* 'Lime Green' (*also below*) adds a tangy twist to a planting of golden marguerites (*Anthemis tinctoria*). Some of the newer nicotiana varieties come in really unusual shades – great for experimenting with wacky color combinations.

STATELY STEMS
Larger than life, *Nicotiana sylvestris* stands head and shoulders above most other nicotianas and has one of the strongest perfumes.

Central crease on each lobe

◄FLOWER SIZE ►
1½in (3.5cm) across

GRABBING THE LIMELIGHT, *right*
It took me several seasons before I grew to like the extraordinary variety 'Lime Green', but now I admire its unusual color, which, magically, appears to glow as dusk falls.

Stems, leaves, and buds are sticky

Daffodils *NARCISSUS*

THE BRIGHT, DANCING heads of daffodils are one of the most welcome sights of spring. They are available in so many different colors and sizes that it is almost impossible not to find at least one that you'd like to grow. Planting fresh bulbs each year guarantees massed color in spring bedding and containers — or let them flower more informally year after year in the border or naturalized in grass. But wherever you use them, plant them in groups — there's no lonelier sight than a solitary daffodil battling a spring storm!

FLOWER SIZE ▶
5in (12cm)
across

SMALL PLEASURES
Grow miniature daffodils such as 'Minnow' in more exposed sites where wind might snap taller stems.

SPRING GOLD
Grown among the pink-purple flowers and attractively spotted leaves of pulmonarias and starlike purple anemones, the classic yellow flowers of 'February Gold' bring a warm, sunny glow to the whole garden in early spring. These medium-sized daffodils are particularly well suited to growing among fairly small perennials.

TRUMPET CALL
Like all full-sized daffodils, 'Bravoure' has one drawback — the dying foliage looks messy. Among herbaceous perennials it is soon hidden, though.

GROWING DAFFODILS

PLANT PROFILE

Bulbs that flower every year. Z 2–9.

- SIZE Most 6–20in (15–50cm); dwarf types can be as tiny as 3in (8cm) tall.
- FLOWER COLORS Orange, yellow, white, cream, pink, green.
- FLOWERING Late winter to midspring.
- SITE Fertile and reasonably moisture-retentive.

Planting Plant in autumn at a depth equal to at least three times the height of the bulb.

Dividing Divide congested clumps of bulbs as necessary (usually every five to seven years).

Plant care Water regularly during dry weather, feed in spring and summer, and divide mature clumps.

After flowering Remove flowers as soon they are over, but leave foliage untouched for at least six weeks after the flowers have faded to ensure healthy flowering next year.

Poor flowering If daffodils become "blind" (produce healthy leaves but few or no flowers), divide and replant, then feed regularly with a high-phosphorus fertilizer throughout the growing period.

My favorites 'Actaea', 'Baby Moon', 'Barrett Browning', 'Bravoure', Narcissus bulbocodium, 'Canaliculatus', N. cyclamineus, 'February Silver', 'Geranium', 'Golden Bells', 'Hawera', 'Ice Follies', 'Ice Wings', 'Jack Snipe', 'Minnow', 'Mount Hood', 'Peeping Tom', N. poeticus var. recurvus, 'Tête-à-tête', 'Thalia'.

If you plant bulbs in slatted pond baskets, you can lift the lot after flowering to let the foliage die back elsewhere.

SIMPLE CHARMS
Surrounding its bright yellow trumpet, the brushed-back petals of 'Jack Snipe' have a windswept charm.

ALPINE FAVORITE
For a miniature alpine-style planting, one of my favorites is Narcissus bulbocodium, the hoop-petticoat daffodil.

SWEET SMELL OF SUCCESS
I adore 'Geranium' for its strong, sweet perfume. The real bonus is that each flower stem bears up to six blooms.

A DAINTY DISH
The yellow cuplike trumpets of 'Canaliculatus' form prominent centerpieces for a ruff of delicate pure white petals.

OLD FAVORITE
It is easy to create your own host of golden daffodils by planting a drift of 'Dutch Master', the classic rich yellow daffodil.

FRILLS AND FLOUNCES
One of the taller daffodils, 'Mount Hood' produces creamy white flowers with flaring, frilly edged trumpets in midspring.

POET'S CORNER
A particular favorite of mine, 'Barrett Browning' has golden yellow trumpets edged with a delicate, bright orange frill.

Flowers with faces

THERE ARE SOME FLOWERS THAT ARE SO EXPRESSIVE THAT THEY GIVE A WHOLE NEW MEANING TO THE TERM "COMPANION PLANTING." THERE'S A FRIENDLY FLOWER WITH A FACE THAT'S just right for almost every situation: clematis to peer down at you from trellises and arches, pretty herbaceous geraniums to invite you into a shady position, and sweet-faced rock roses and jaunty poppies tempting you over to a sunny corner. But without a doubt, the violas and pansies – among the best-known and best-loved flowers of all time – present the widest range of expressions, from wide-eyed innocence to a broad grin and even a grumpy scowl. Grow a few of my favorites here, and there will always be bright faces to to say hello to whenever you go into the garden – and unlike your family and neighbors, they won't answer back!

"Flamboyant flowers as fine as tissue paper guarantee poppies an entrée into the best flower borders."

POPPIES, PAGES 110–111

Left POPPIES (PP.110–111), IRRESISTIBLE IN THEIR SIMPLICITY AND ELEGANCE

107

Spring anemones *ANEMONE*

THE PERSONALITIES OF anemones fall into two distinct camps. Some, such as *Anemone blanda*, are the picture of fresh, daisy-faced innocence, while others, notably *A. coronaria*, are sultry, brazen beauties in rich, solid colors. Most of the spring-flowering anemones grow from knobby tubers or have swollen, fleshy type of roots known as rhizomes. Plant them in groups or miniature drifts – they look distinctly sad when planted singly.

GROWING ANEMONES

PLANT PROFILE

Perennials. *A. coronaria*, *A. fulgens* Z 8–10; *A. blanda*, *A. nemorosa*, *A. ranunculoides* Z 4–8.

• SIZE Most 6–12in (15–30cm).

• FLOWER COLORS Red, blue, purple, lilac, pink, white, cream.

• FLOWERING Most early to midspring.

• SITE Well-drained soil, in part shade or sun. *A. nemorosa* prefers a shady spot.

Planting tubers Don't be put off by the shriveled appearance of anemone tubers – despite their miserable appearance, they will produce plants! Before planting, soak the tubers first in warm (not hot) water for a few hours, perhaps overnight. They will swell up, and a much higher percentage will go on to produce good, sturdy plants. Never allow tubers to soak for more than 24 hours, and be ready to plant them out as soon as you remove them from the water. Plant them about 1½–2in (4–5cm) deep.

Dividing Separate offsets from tubers or divide rhizomatous clumps in late summer or early autumn.

Naturalizing The woodland anemones *A. blanda* and *A. nemorosa* are perfect for naturalizing beneath shrubs and trees. Plant in a random fashion and allow them to spread.

My favorites *Anemone blanda* 'Ingramii', *A. b.* Radar', *A. b.* 'White Splendour'; *A. coronaria* De Caen Group 'Mister Fokker' and 'The Bride', *A. c.* St. Brigid Group 'Lord Lieutenant'; *A.* × *fulgens*; *A. nemorosa*, *A. n.* 'Allenii', *A. n.* 'Robinsoniana; *A. ranunculoides*; *A. sylvestris*. For excellent cut flowers, try *A. coronaria* De Caen and St. Brigid Groups.

DARK-EYED BEAUTIES
The De Caen and St. Brigid groups are full of varieties in jewel-like colors; they make superb cut flowers.

◀ FLOWER SIZE
3 ¼in (8cm) across

SAFE HAVEN
Grow *Anemone coronaria* in a sheltered spot, and the display will last for several weeks in spring. Avoid excessive water during the summer.

Anemone nemorosa is easy to naturalize under shrubs or trees, but you must avoid mowing off the foliage, so choose areas of sparse grass or woodland-style areas.

For anemone flowers later in the year, grow the tall, clump-forming herbaceous perennials known as Japanese anemones (see pp.156–157), which flower from the end of the summer until midautumn.

WEDDING BELLE
The inner petals of *Anemone coronaria* De Caen Group 'The Bride' are subtly tinged with pale lime green toward a yellow-green center.

LOOKING GOOD
Although quite small, each bright magenta flower of *Anemone blanda* 'Radar' has a central white "eye" that seems to stare right back at you.

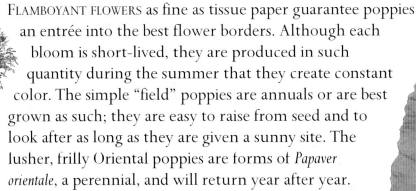

Poppies *PAPAVER*

FLAMBOYANT FLOWERS as fine as tissue paper guarantee poppies an entrée into the best flower borders. Although each bloom is short-lived, they are produced in such quantity during the summer that they create constant color. The simple "field" poppies are annuals or are best grown as such; they are easy to raise from seed and to look after as long as they are given a sunny site. The lusher, frilly Oriental poppies are forms of *Papaver orientale*, a perennial, and will return year after year.

BRIGHT AND BUBBLY
Iceland poppies, such as *Papaver croceum* 'Champagne Bubbles' here, come in a mixture of yellows and oranges and are sometimes lightly scented.

OPPOSITES ATTRACT
The stark contrast between the crimson-black center and the papery white petals of *Papaver orientale* 'Black and White' creates a minimalist impact: these are truly monochrome flowers.

DELICATE PINKS
The pink petals of *Papaver orientale* 'Cedric Morris' look as light as a puff of air, set against gray-green foliage. All varieties of *P. orientale* can be divided after the leaves die down or in spring.

SPELLBOUND
It's no wonder that *Papaver rhoeas* 'Mother of Pearl' is also known as 'Fairy Wings', for this relative of the corn poppy has a fairylike quality. They are easily raised from seed and will often self-seed.

GROWING POPPIES

PLANT PROFILE

Annuals and perennials; some short-lived perennials are best grown as annuals. Z 2–9.

- SIZE Most 18–36in (45–90cm).
- FLOWER COLORS Red, orange, yellow, purple, pink, white.
- FLOWERING Throughout summer.
- SITE Well-drained soil, in full sun.

Planting Perennial poppies perform well when mulched with compost on planting and each spring.

Sowing seeds Raise perennials from seed sown in pots in a cold frame toward the end of autumn or in early spring. Annual poppies are almost impossible to transplant and, with the exception of *Papaver croceum,* they simply die if you attempt it, so always sow seed as thinly as possible directly in the flowering site.

Self-seeding Poppies are prolific self-seeding plants, so look out for seedlings close to parent plants and try to keep a few, even if they are not in the "ideal" place.

Flower care Regular deadheading as soon as the flowers drop their petals prolongs the flowering period.

My favorites Annuals: *Papaver commutatum* 'Ladybird', *P. rhoeas*, *P. somniferum.*
Short-lived perennials: *P. croceum* (syn. *P. nudicaule*) 'Champagne Bubbles', *P. c.* 'Red Sails'.
Perennials: *P. orientale*, *P. o.* 'Allegro Viva', *P. o.* 'Beauty Queen', *P. o.* 'Curlilocks', *P. o.* 'Mrs. Perry', *P. o.* 'Perry's White', *P. o.* 'Picotée'.

Allow a few poppies to form seedheads, which look good on the plant and are striking in dried flower arrangements.

◀ FLOWER SIZE
3in (7.5cm)
across

EASTERN PROMISE

With its scarlet-orange, cup-shaped flowers, *Papaver orientale* brightens up any sunny spot in late spring. Even its dark throat can't make it the slightest bit somber!

Subtle gradations of color banding across each petal

SCARLET AND BLACK, *left*

The unmistakable petal patterning of *Papaver somniferum* resembles that of the classic Flanders poppy, found in abundance growing wild in the countryside of northern France.

IMPRESSIONISTS' DREAM, *right*

Poppies are seen at their dreamiest grown in sizeable drifts. Each flower may not be long-lasting, but they are produced in such profusion throughout the summer and are so beautiful that I always try to find a space for a scattering of seeds.

Rock roses *Cistus*

ALSO KNOWN AS SUN ROSES, rock roses are among the most reliable and beautiful plants to grow in hot, sunny climates where soil moisture is scarce. Each one of their delicate, papery, roselike flowers lasts for only a single day, but they are produced in such numbers that these bushy plants still provide a long show of color throughout the summer months. For real impact, grow several identical plants in a group. If you garden fairly close to the sea, you can still grow these fragile beauties, because in mild climates they stand up well to salt-laden winds.

STRIKE SILVER
Each individual rock rose bloom fades fast, but there are always masses of buds waiting to replace them. This is 'Silver Pink'.

FLIGHT OF FANCY
The petals of many rock roses remind me of the wings of a newly emerged butterfly, crinkled like scrunched silk.

FLOWER SIZE ▶
2¼in (5.5cm) across

Flower buds occur in clusters and open one by one

Rock roses are ideal container plants, especially in very sunny positions where other plants would soon suffer from drought.

Rock roses make an excellent groundcover scrambling over dry, sunny banks. Try the low-growing Cistus × dansereaui 'Decumbens'.

Shelter rock roses from cold, biting winds.

SHOCKING PINK, *right*
Cistus (here *C. × purpureus*) make lovely, loose, informal mounds, ideal for cascading over the edges of slightly raised beds.

GROWING ROCK ROSES

PLANT PROFILE

Shrubby perennials, hardy only in warm gardens and in protected positions; they can be badly damaged by frost. Z 8–10.

- SIZE Most 2–4ft (60–120cm), some to 9ft (2.7m).
- FLOWER COLORS Pink, white, often with blotches.
- FLOWERING Late spring to midsummer.
- SITE Sandy and very free-draining soil in full sun.

Sowing seeds You can sow in spring, in a cold frame, for plants to set out the following spring. Hybrids do not breed true from seed.

Planting Mid- to late spring. Add extra grit to improve drainage. Rock roses resent being moved, so try to choose the right spot the first time!

Cuttings You can take semiripe, heeled cuttings in midsummer, using nonflowering shoots 3–4in (7.5–10cm) long. Root them in a propagating case. Keep young plants under cover over winter and plant out in spring.

Pruning Only prune established cistus if absolutely necessary. Once young plants have finished flowering, you can pinch them back to encourage plenty of bushy growth and to prevent them from becoming straggly. Once an older plant has become straggly, it is best discarded because it will not respond well to pruning, usually dying back further.

My favorites Cistus × aquilarii 'Maculatus', C. × cyprius, C. × dansereaui 'Decumbens', C. × hybridus, C. incanus subsp. creticus, C. ladinifer, C. 'Peggy Sammons', C. × pulverulentus 'Sunset', C. × purpureus, C. × skanbergii.

BIRD CALL, *right*
With its contrasting crimson eye at the base of each white petal, *Cistus × dansereaui* 'Decumbens' reminds me of an exotically feathered bird. This superb, low-growing shrub attracts attention all through summer.

Hellebores *HELLEBORUS*

THE SHY, SUBTLE, BELL-LIKE FLOWERS of hellebores put them among my most treasured winter-garden plants. Choose carefully, and you can have hellebores in bloom from late winter until late spring. These moisture-loving plants will thrive in part shade, and some will even grow in full shade, brightening up the gloomiest corners of the garden. Many of these perennials also have robust, attractive foliage, bringing year-round interest to the border.

PERFECT STRANGER, *above*
Hellebores hybridize so freely that their offspring may never be given official names. The results are often lovely, as here, and well worth growing.

FRECKLE FACE, *left*
Many of the most appealing hellebores have delicately freckled petals, such as this *Helleborus orientalis*.

GREEN GODDESS
The unusual green-flowered *Helleborus cyclophyllus* is one of my favorites, not least for the bonus of its delicate scent.

WHITE CHRISTMAS
The classic *Helleborus niger*, best known as the Christmas rose, produces beautiful white flowers sometimes flushed with pink.

GROWING HELLEBORES

PLANT PROFILE

Perennials. Z 4–9.

• SIZE 18–36in (45–90cm).

• FLOWER COLORS Green, purple, lilac, pink, white, cream; some may be freckled with contrasting colors.

• FLOWERING Throughout late winter to late spring.

• SITE A moist soil in partial shade. Once established, leave them in peace because they resent root disturbance.

Soil Unless you can improve dry or thin soil so that it becomes more moisture-retentive it is not worth growing hellebores: they will not thrive. Improve soil by incorporating well-rotted compost before planting.

Sowing seeds Saving and sowing seed from hellebores is a great way of getting interesting plants, since the offspring will not be the same as the parents but often have lovely colors and markings. Sow ripe seed taken in early to midsummer and plant in sandy soil mix in a cold frame. It will take three years before you have flowering-sized plants.

Dividing You can divide mature clumps in autumn, but keep plenty of soil around the roots.

Watering Keep hellebores well watered during dry weather.

Fantastic flowers Cut off the leaves of *H. orientalis* in late winter to really show the flowers off at their best. New leaves will grow in spring.

Leaf damage The fungal disease hellebore leafspot may do a lot of damage. Control it by picking off affected leaves and, if necessary, spray with a suitable fungicide.

My favorites *Helleborus* Ashwood Garden hybrids; *H. atrorubens*; *H. foetidus* 'Wester Flisk'; *H. lividus*; *H. niger*, *H. n.* 'Potter's Wheel'; *H. orientalis*. With its pale, almost emerald-green flowers, *H. argutifolius* looks splendid interplanted with *Iris reticulata*. *H. cyclophyllus* has the bonus of perfume from its yellowish green flowers. *H. orientalis* is lovely planted among a drift of snowdrops, perhaps beneath a favorite tree or shrub. Try combining *H. foetidus* with winter-flowering heathers.

FLOWER SIZE ▶
2¹⁄₂in (6.5cm)
across

MYSTERY GUEST
Here's more proof that it pays to
keep and grow on any seedling
hellebores you may find in the
garden. Although plants may take
several years to reach flowering
size, with results like this it
is surely well worth
the wait.

*Dark purple flecks
are set against pink-
flushed petals*

*Prominent golden
stamens are grouped
in a central cluster*

A ROSE FOR SPRING, *left*
From late winter to late spring
Helleborus orientalis, the evocatively
named (if often rather premature)
Lenten Rose produces white, greenish
cream, or almost velvety wine-red
flowers. But even before it blooms,
this clump-forming hellebore is well
worth growing for its large,
handsome, shiny green leaves.

*Hellebores make gorgeous cut
flowers, so always grow a few
extra plants just for cutting.
I recommend Helleborus
argutifolius, H. atrorubens,
H. foetidus (don't crush the
leaves, since they give off an
unpleasant smell)
and H. niger. .*

*Helleborus foetidus is ideal
for very shady sites; it thrives
in such locations.*

Viola and pansies *VIOLA*

DARK MYSTERY
Among plant enthusiasts in particular there is often a lot of fuss and intrigue about "black" flowers – grow *Viola* 'Molly Sanderson' and you will soon understand why.

PERHAPS IT'S THEIR bright, often impish faces that make violas and pansies so appealing, but I'm sure that they are also popular because they are just so simple to grow. Both easy and eager to please, they'll put on a good display in most conditions, flowering continuously in cooler weather. If you choose winter-flowering types, they will not only perform well throughout winter and spring but may carry on through early summer, if given the chance. You can use these plants in almost any situation – baskets, windowboxes, beds, borders, and for edging and in rock gardens.

VIOLET EYES
For a simple, subtle combination, *Viola cornuta* 'Purple Duet' uses two shades of mauve to offset its contrasting bright yellow eye.

BLEND OF BLUE
Not all violas have sharply defined markings: the flowers of *Viola cornuta* 'Blueberry Cream' have beautifully graded color.

MARKS OF DISTINCTION, *above and below*
Like little cat's whiskers, these striking pollen guidelines are a feature of many varieties.

JEWEL BRIGHT, *above*
Many pansies come in mixed colors. Here, *Viola* × *wittrockiana* Forerunner Series creates a stained-glass effect.

◀ FLOWER SIZE
¾in (2cm) across

GROWING VIOLAS AND PANSIES

PLANT PROFILE

Annuals or perennials for almost year-round displays; cold adaptability varies. Violas Z 7–9; pansies Z 5–9.

- SIZE 2–12in (5–30cm).
- FLOWER COLORS Red, orange, yellow, blue, purple, lilac, pink, white, cream, brown.
- FLOWERING Depends upon climate and variety.
- SITE Ideally, well-drained soil, in slight shade.

Soil Violas and pansies grow well in almost any soil, although they prefer a well-drained spot. They will not last as long in heavy clay.

Position A slightly shaded spot is best, but they also perform well in full sun. If conditions are too gloomy, they tend to grow taller and become slightly leggy.

Sowing seed Easy to raise from seed, and a huge selection is available. The seeds should germinate well in a cold frame in summer or in a shady part of the garden protected from birds.

Flower care Deadhead regularly to ensure a plentiful and long-lasting display of flowers. Leave one or two seedheads to develop if you want to raise a few plants from seed. If plants become straggly, give them a trim with a pair of scissors to encourage denser growth and, often, more flowers.

My favorites *V. cornuta* 'Chantryland'; 'Etain'; 'Jackanapes'; 'Molly Sanderson'; *V. tricolor*, *V. t.* 'Bowles' Black'; *V. × wittrockiana* Crystal Bowl Series, *V. × w.* Forerunner Series., *V. × w.* Imperial Series, *V. × w.* Universal Series.

Violas and pansies are widely available as bedding plants, ready to plant out for fast-growing color.

Sharply contrasting blotches of color define the "face"

TRIED AND TESTED

For either winter or spring color, pansies – here, *Viola × wittrockiana* 'Turbo Red' (*above*), 'White Blotch' (*below*) and 'Violet Blotch' (*right*) – can be relied upon to put on a good display.

Central area is covered in soft down

Purple markings form the outline of a butterfly

◄ FLOWER SIZE
2in (5cm)
across

Clematis *CLEMATIS*

EASY TO GROW, VERSATILE, and incredibly pretty, clematis must easily be the most popular of the flowering climbers. They look terrific grown traditionally, clambering up walls and fences, but I squeeze more into the garden scrambling through trees, shrubs, or other climbers – even as a ground-cover to create a carpet of color. The large-flowered types shown here flower during summer, but by choosing carefully, you can use clematis to bring vertical color to your garden almost all year.

BIG ATTRACTION
From late spring to early summer, the large blue-purple flowers and cream anthers of 'H. F. Young' are impossible to miss. As with other clematis that flower at a similar time, prompt deadheading encourages a second flush of flowers in late summer or early autumn.

STATE PRESENCE
Reliable and prolific, 'The President' has large, rich purple flowers in bloom from early summer until early autumn.

FADED GRANDEUR
The early-flowering 'Bees' Jubilee' prefers partial shade. The flower color fades with age or if grown in too sunny a position.

ABOUT TOWN
To avoid leaf scorch, grow 'Ville de Lyon' through an evergreen shrub. Bright carmine flowers appear in mid- to late summer.

GROWING CLEMATIS

PLANT PROFILE

Perennials. Z 4–9.

- SIZE Most 8–20ft (2.4–6m)
- FLOWER COLORS Red, yellow, blue, purple, lilac, pink, white, cream.
- FLOWERING Most spring to late summer, depending on type.
- SITE Position in sun or part shade, always with the base of the plant in shade. A neutral loamy soil is ideal, but they can do well in alkaline soil.

Planting Set the crown of the plant 3in (7.5cm) beneath the soil surface. Keep the roots cool by deep planting and by covering the soil around the root area with decorative stones or another plant.

Cuttings Take semiripe cuttings in midsummer, 4–5in (10–12cm) long, with at least two buds at the base. To root, they need a propagating case set at 59–64°F (15–18°C).

Pruning Varies greatly. Prune *C. montana* and other small-flowered spring clematis only if they become too big. For large-flowered hybrids

flowering in late spring/early summer, prune lightly after flowering, removing weak and dead wood and cutting stems back to healthy buds. Prune clematis that flower later in summer and in autumn by cutting back hard to about 10in (25cm) of ground level in late winter or early spring.

My favorites *Clematis alpina* 'Pink Flamingo', *C. a.* 'Ruby'; *C. armandii*; 'Blue Belle'; *C. cirrhosa* 'Freckles'; *C. florida* 'Sieboldii'; 'Gypsy Queen'; 'Hagley Hybrid'; 'Henryi'; 'Marie Boisselot'; *C. montana* 'Elizabeth', *C. m.* var. *rubens*; 'Nelly Moser'; 'Niobe'.

Clematis look at their most natural when allowed to scramble through a tree, shrub, or hedge and can add an extra season of interest to their host plant. Initially, train the stems toward the trunk on stakes or trellis, then allow the clematis to do as it pleases.

Twining leaf-stalks readily attach to support

FLOWER SIZE ▶
3–4in (7.5–10cm) across

PRETTY MISS, *above*
Beautiful, glossy white flowers cover 'Miss Bateman' in early summer; like many of the large-flowered hybrids, she often produces a second flush in early autumn.

PROTECTIVE CAMOUFLAGE, *left*
As clematis age, they often become bare around the base, but planting a small shrub in front disguises this shortcoming and also gives the roots some shade – which clematis need – in sunny spots.

119

Geraniums GERANIUM

WITH THEIR SIMPLE, unostentatious beauty, perennial geraniums always look, to me, a little surprised by their recent surge in popularity. But in my view, few plants work harder to deserve it more: there are geraniums that will be "good doers" for almost any site; they get on well with, and usually flatter, most other garden plants; and they flower their little hearts out for months and months. What is more, the foliage is pretty and in many develops lovely autumnal tints as the seasons change; be sure to position these where you can enjoy the turning colors.

Faded flowers resemble the head of a crane, hence "cranesbill"

TRICK OF THE LIGHT
The pure purple petals of *Geranium himalayense* 'Gravetye' form simple disks of color that seem to light up when the sun is behind them: fantastic next to yellow flowers.

IN A DISTINCTIVE VEIN
The purple-pink flowers of 'Salome' are given character by the dark purple markings etched on the almost luminous petals, offset by pale green leaves.

SHADES OF SUMMER
A pretty plant for a shady spot, *Geranium phaeum* has petals so delicate that they could have been cut from finest silk. In contrast, the prominent stamens shout out for attention.

SILVERY STUNNERS
White-flowered varieties such as this *Geranium phaeum* 'Album' look stunning surrounded by the silvery white-variegated foliage of *Lamium maculatum* 'Beacon Silver' or 'White Nancy'.

PERFECT PARTNERS
Plant violet-flowered geraniums under a pink rose – here, *Geranium × magnificum* with *Rosa* 'Fantin-Latour'. Roses often develop bare lower stems, which the geraniums will hide.

GROWING GERANIUMS

PLANT PROFILE

Perennials. Z 4–8.

- SIZE 6–42in (15–105cm).
- FLOWER COLORS White, pink, purple, lilac, blue.
- FLOWERING Early summer to late autumn.
- SITE Some geraniums do well in full shade, but most prefer either sun or part shade. Unfussy about soil, except for alpine geraniums, which need good drainage.

Support Use twiggy sticks to subtly support taller varieties.

Repeating flowers Cut back after flowering to encourage dense growth and a second flush of flowers.

Division Divide established clumps at the end of the summer or in spring.

Cuttings You can take root cuttings from *Geranium pratense* and *G. sanguineum*; both have thick roots.

Sowing seeds Species come true from seed. Sow in spring in a cold frame and plant out in autumn.

My favorites 'Ann Folkard', *Geranium cinereum* 'Ballerina', *G. gracile*, *G. × oxonianum* 'Wargrave Pink', *G. pratense* f. *albiflorum*, 'Salome', *G. sanguineum*, *G. sylvaticum* 'Album'. For edging a large border, 'Johnson's Blue' is ideal, with a compact, moundlike habit and blue flowers. *G. × oxonianum* 'Walter's Gift' and *G. phaeum* 'Samobor' have particularly attractive foliage. The magenta-purple flowers of *G. psilostemon* look fantastic with buttercups or mingling with *Rosa* 'Maigold', which gives the stems support. *G. himalayense* 'Gravetye', *G. macrorrhizum* 'Album', *G. phaeum*, and *G. p.* 'Album' are good in shade.

Low-growing, compact geraniums such as Geranium clarkei 'Kashmir White' make pretty, informal edging.

Look closely to see the etched lines that guide insects toward the pollen

◄ FLOWER SIZE
1¼in (3cm)
across

Stems may need support; twiggy sticks are ideal for these informal plants

REACH FOR THE SKY
The lavender-pink flowers of *Geranium maculatum* 'Chatto' light up the partly shaded sites it enjoys. Taller geraniums such as this often need staking, particularly in shade, where they usually grow more vigorously.

PART
THREE

PERFECT PLANTING

Right plant, right place

MATCHING A PLANT TO THE conditions you can offer it makes good garden sense. Put a plant where it naturally feels at home and it is more likely to thrive, with little work from you. By slightly altering the conditions, you can bend the rules, for example by incorporating coarse organic matter into the soil to improve moisture retention, by adding horticultural sand to beds or planting holes to improve drainage, or by planting a shrub to create shelter for a shade-loving plant. If you take care, amending your site to suit a plant's needs will work, though the chances are that you will need to lavish more care on a plant growing in "artificial" surroundings than one thriving in a naturally suitable site.

A GREEN AND PLEASANT PLACE
There isn't as wide a choice of flowering plants for shade as in sun, but you can cheat to enhance the effect: here, pale epimediums are boosted by the white-splashed foliage of shade-loving hostas.

GARDEN CHECKLIST

Always check the requirements of a plant against what your garden can offer before you buy. Point-of-sale material and plant labels should provide you with most of the information you need, and don't hesitate to ask for advice. Points you should consider include:

1 The soil pH or acidity: some plants may discolor or even die in acidic soil.

2 Sunlight needs: in shady conditions sun-loving plants will produce fewer blooms.

3 Moisture content of soil: too wet or too free-draining may cause root death.

4 Overall climate: will the plant survive your winter, or will it need shelter?

5 Open or sheltered site: in exposed areas, winds in particular may be drying.

6 The exposure: does the site face north, south? How much sun does it get, and when?

7 Planting against a wall: it may provide protection, but will rain reach the plant?

8 Sloping ground: tends to be drier at the top, becoming wetter toward the base.

PLANT CHECKLIST

Having satisfied yourself that your garden or site will suit the plant you'd like to grow, don't forget to consider these two essential points:

SIZE
Check the mature size of the plant. It may look small and well behaved when you first see it, but appearances can be deceiving. Before you know it, it may grow far too big, shading or swamping other plants nearby, blocking a path, or shading the lawn. It may be possible to prune the plant to keep it to the required dimensions, but some plants respond better to this than others. Pruning could ruin its natural shape or even cause it to die back.

SAFETY
Some plants are known to be potentially hazardous: they may cause poisoning, mild gastric upsets, or adverse skin reactions of varying severity. The whole plant may be a risk or it may have seasonal features, such as poisonous berries, that pose a threat. If the garden is to be used by children, be especially vigilant about the plants that you choose to grow. Similarly, plants with thorns or irritant hairs may be better suited to out-of-the way places.

FINDING THE RIGHT SITE, *right*
Moist soil, dappled shade, and fairly
humid air suit plants such as these
ligularias, astilbes, and mimulus perfectly,
creating a gorgeous display with little
effort on your part. Plants less at home in
these conditions may become drawn and
leggy, fail to flower, and be more prone to
pests and diseases. Some plants tolerate a
range of conditions: the astilbes, for
instance (*also below*), will grow in boggy
soil in sun, or in drier (but still moisture-
retentive) soil in shade, so they could be
used as linking plants to create continuity
between plantings in different areas
of the garden.

What plant where?

TO BE HONEST, it's hard not to behave like a kid let loose in a candy store when you're at the garden center or nursery. But before you succumb to love at first sight in every direction, check that the plants that have caught your eye are suitable for your garden, especially for challenging areas — deep shade, a wet or dry spot — or you may be in for a disappointment. Turn less-than-perfect conditions to your advantage by choosing plants that will positively thrive, not just survive, in them.

SUNNY AND DRY
Hot sun, free-draining soil, sloping ground, and windy conditions can all create a dry site. These *Gazania* 'Orange Beauty' positively thrive in a dry soil and love basking in the sun.

MOVEABLE FEAST, *above*
If your garden has mostly hard surfaces, or you simply want instant color, plants in containers are the answer. Here, begonias add seasonal color.

SOIL SOLUTIONS, *right*
Some people worry about having an alkaline soil, but there are plenty of smashing plants that thrive in limy soils. These *Physostegia virginiana* and anemones couldn't look happier.

CURTAIN CALL, *above*
Blank vertical surfaces cry out for a climber or wall shrub. Here, the richly perfumed blooms of honeysuckle clamber around a window, so its perfume can be enjoyed both inside and out.

Corydalis
flexuosa

COOL BEAUTY, *left*
Shady areas need luminous colors. These blue *Corydalis flexuosa* and white dicentras really freshen up the lovely hues and textures of subtle foliage plants.

WATER WAYS, *right*
A damp corner or boggy ground alongside a water feature offer the ideal conditions for lush planting. Here, swaths of the golden yellow marsh marigold (*Caltha palustris*) are complemented by variegated iris foliage.

Plants with a purpose

WE CHOOSE PLANTS for all sorts of reasons. Often it simply comes down to pure visual appeal, and there's nothing wrong with that (as long as they'll be happy in the spot you have in mind). But wouldn't it be wonderful if that same plant also smelled divine, brought clouds of butterflies into the garden, or was ideal for cutting? The flowering plants I've chosen on the following pages aren't just for solving problem sites; they all have added value – the bonus of beautiful foliage, for example – to repay your care.

EASY PICKINGS, *above*
What could be better than a plant that looks good in the flower border and can also be cut and used indoors in flower arrangements? These Chinese lanterns (*Physalis alkekengi* var. *franchetii*) are grown for their bright orange, bell-shaped seedheads, which look superb in dried flower decorations.

DOWN TO EARTH, *left*
Bare soil has little appeal and usually attracts weeds in no time, making it both uninteresting and hard work. Using groundcover plants can transform such a patch into a carpet of color and texture. Here, the rosette-forming *Tiarella cordifolia* combines pretty flowers with attractive, dense foliage.

GREEN DREAM, *above*
Most plants are in leaf for a much greater proportion of the year than they are in flower, so anything that has distinctive foliage is of interest. The flowers of *Alchemilla mollis* are incredibly pretty, but the grayish green, scalloped leaves are so gorgeous that it would be worth using even if it never flowered.

BUTTERFLY BALL, *above and left*
No garden is complete without its quota of busy, friendly insects. Above, a small tortoiseshell butterfly briefly feeds on a sedum. Many flowers attract beneficial insects. These *Monarda didyma* 'Cambridge Scarlet' (*left*) with their crazy mophead flowers and dazzling color not only brighten up a late summer border; as far as butterflies and bees are concerned, someone has kindly laid out a feast of nectar.

FLOWER FILLERS, *above*
Quick-growing annuals that are easily raised from seed are an excellent way to fill gaps in new or established plantings. Here, masses of pink *Lavatera trimestris* add to the glorious but more subtle colors of nearby *Anemone × hybrida* and a pale pink rose.

SCENT TO PLEASE
Thymes are an excellent value: these tough little plants soften path edges and actually reward the odd careless footfall with a burst of aromatic fragrance from their bruised leaves. Here they spread themselves invitingly in front of a garden bench backed by cool blue catmints.

Scented flowers

FOR ME, A GARDEN isn't complete unless it includes plenty of scented flowers and aromatic foliage. The combination of flowers, foliage, and perfume is a heady cocktail, and by choosing carefully you can enjoy scent in the evening as well as in the day – heaven!

OTHER FLOWERS FOR SCENT

Wallflowers (*Cheiranthus cheiri*) pp.154–155
Sweet peas (*Lathyrus odoratus*) pp.56–57
Lilies (*Lilium*) pp.62–63
Honeysuckle (*Lonicera*) pp.134–135
Daffodils (*Narcissus*) pp.104–105
Nicotianas (*Nicotiana*) pp.102–103

SWEET NATURED
Forming a neat mound, *Heliotropium arborescens* 'Marine', like other heliotropes, brings rich color and a vanilla-like perfume into the garden in summer.

BELLES OF THE BORDER
Stocks come in widely different shapes, sizes, and colors – here, the compact *Matthiola incana* Cinderella Series – and all of them have a strong, rich scent.

PLANT	SIZE	APPEARANCE
LILY-OF-THE-VALLEY *Convallaria majalis* Z 2–7	H 6–8in (15–20cm) S 6in (15cm)	This vigorous, rapidly spreading peren creates a fragrant carpet of arching flo stems draped with tiny bell-like flowe in white or pale pink. They are produc from mid- to late spring.
GAS PLANT *Dictamnus albus* Z 3–8	H 26in (65cm) S 10in (25cm)	Summer and a tang of citrus go togethe so find a sunny spot for this long-lived perennial with lemon-scented foliage a flowers. Striking spikes of star-shaped flowers appear in early summer.
FREESIAS *Freesia* Z 10–11	H 12–18in (30–45cm) S 3–4in (7.5–10cm)	Giving off a sweet, warm, and spicy sce the delicate sprays of funnel-shaped fl in white or shades of purple, red, orang blue, yellow, cream, or pink are a defini hit in late spring and early summer.
HELIOTROPE *Heliotropium arborescens* Annual	H 18–24in (45–60cm) S 8–10in (20–25cm)	Perfect for containers, the flowers, in w or shades of purple, violet, or blue, hav delightful perfume and are packed into large heads throughout the summer. I grown as an annual.
SWEET ROCKET *Hesperis matronalis* Z 4–9	H 3ft (90cm) S 12in (30cm)	Sweet rocket has pink, white, or purpl fragrant flower spikes that appear in ea and midsummer. Its fragrance, althoug good in the day, is sublime once the su goes down.
HYACINTHS *Hyacinthus* Z 5–9	H 8–10in (20–25cm) S 4–6in (10–15cm)	You either love or hate the pervasive s of hyacinths. The dense flower spikes p with fleshy, bell-shaped flowers in whi shades of pink, blue, violet, salmon, yel or cream are spring classics.
STOCKS *Matthiola* Annual	H 12–20in (30–50cm) S 12in (30cm)	Dense, blowsy, sweet-scented flower s bloom in late spring to midsummer. Flowers may be single, double, or a mi of both on one spike and come in whi shades of pink, lilac, mauve, or purple
EVENING PRIMROSE *Oenothera biennis* Z 4–8	H 3ft (90cm) S 16in (40cm)	The fragrant, fragile-looking yellow fl of this biennial bloom from early sum until the middle of autumn. Flowers as the sun sets – perfect by a terrace w you sit or eat in the evenings.
GARDEN PHLOX *Phlox paniculata* Z 4–8	H 12–36in (30–90cm) S 3ft (90cm)	An essential ingredient of any herbace border in summer, the showy pink, re orange, lilac, bluish mauve, or white flowerheads, up to 6in (15cm) across, a very sweet fragrance that hangs in th
THYMES *Thymus* Z 4–9	H 2–10in (5–25cm) S 6–18in (15–45cm)	The pungent, aromatic foliage of these creeping evergreen perennials is toppe with tiny white, pink, or purple flowe midsummer. Some forms have attract variegated or woolly foliage.

POWER PACK
Sheer strength of perfume is combined here with the intensely purplish blue flowers of *Hyacinthus orientalis* 'Blue Jacket'.

SITE	CULTIVATION	HINTS AND TIPS
A site in dappled shade or in full sun; soil should be moist.	Plant crowns in autumn or early spring, just beneath the surface. Mulch regularly with leafmold to keep the soil moist. Divide established plants in autumn.	• For pale pink flowers, choose *C. majalis* var. *rosea*. • For superb creamy white and green-striped foliage, choose 'Albostriata'. The leaves make a lovely edging for the flowers when arranged in a tiny vase or posy.
A sunny site with free-draining, ideally alkaline soil.	Plant container-grown plants in a spot where you can enjoy their aroma. It resents disturbance, so avoid moving it once established.	• *D. albus* var. *purpureus* has scented pink flowers streaked with purple. • The volatile oil produced by the flowers and leaves may occasionally cause skin irritation. • Use the starry seedheads in dried arrangements.
Choose a sheltered, sunny spot with a well-drained soil.	Freesias can't survive much cold. Plant corms about 1¼in (3cm) deep, ideally in early spring. Lift in autumn, and store in a dry, cool, but frost-free place.	• If necessary, when planting incorporate sand to improve drainage. Provide twiggy sticks for support in windy areas. • They may be grown indoors in pots in a cool, bright spot for spring bloom.
Well-drained soil and full sun.	Sow seeds in late winter at 61–64°F (16–18°C) or buy as small plants. Plant out after the frosts are over. Take under cover or discard at the end of summer.	• Choose the dwarf 'Marine' for plants with rich purple flowers that grow only 12in (30cm) high. • Overwinter heliotropes in a cool, frost-free porch or greenhouse. Trim back hard in spring. • Heliotropes thrive in containers.
Thrives in poor soil and loves some shade.	Best grown as an annual or short-lived perennial. Sweet rocket prefers a well-drained soil, so incorporate leafmold or compost when planting.	• Replace plants every two or three years or grow as an annual. • Divide established plants in spring or take basal cuttings in late spring or early summer. They usually self-sow.
Best in a well-drained soil in sun.	Plant the bulbs in containers or borders between late summer and late autumn. Plant 4in (10cm) deep and 6–8in (15–20cm) apart.	• After their first year, the bulbs tend to produce rather sparsely covered flower spikes. Plant new bulbs each year if you want thick spikes. • Aphids and slugs may be a problem, so control these pests if necessary.
Select a site in sun or part shade with fertile, moist soil.	Available as young plants, or sow seed direct outside in mid-spring (as annuals) or early/midsummer and then overwinter (as biennials in Zones 7–8).	• Taller varieties may need some support; they can become top-heavy. • For quick results, choose *M. incana* 'Seven Week' or 'Ten Week', which should flower in about the stated number of weeks after the seed is sown.
Needs plenty of sun and well-drained, preferably sandy soil.	Best planted in either autumn or spring and kept well watered during spring and summer. If growing from seed, sow direct in spring.	• Plants may tend to flop, so subtle staking with stakes or twiggy branches is often necessary. • A rampant self-seeder once established in the garden: be prepared to weed out numerous seedlings, or it may become a pest.
Choose a sunny or part-shaded site in fertile, moisture-retentive soil.	Plant in autumn or spring, incorporating extra organic matter. Divide established clumps every three or four years and replant on a fresh site.	• Powdery mildew disease is a common and damaging problem, especially toward the end of the summer on plants that have become too dry. • 'White Admiral' and 'Starfire' are my particular favorites, great for attracting bees and butterflies.
Require a free-draining soil and a very sunny spot.	Plant in early summer or in spring. After flowering, give a gentle "haircut" to keep plants dense. Replace plants every few years if they become straggly.	• Thymes are perfect for growing in cracks and crevices in paving, around steps, or on a terrace. • Interesting varieties are *T.* × *citriodorus* (lemon thyme), 'Aureus' (variegated yellow foliage), and 'Silver Queen' (variegated cream and white).

STARRY-EYED
Delicate, starry flowers are carried in compact spikes by *Dictamnus albus* var. *purpureus*, forming a scented, pink-white haze above the plant.

HEAVEN SCENT
Freesia is the one scented flower I cannot be without, in the garden or in the home. The combination of its graceful shape, rich yet delicate colors, and fantastic fragrance is irresistible.

Fast-growing flowers

THE PLANTS HERE are ideal for filling the odd unexpected gap or for making a new border or garden quickly seem more established. Not only will the garden soon look better, but you will also feel that you have really achieved something in a relatively short period of time.

OTHER FAST-GROWING FLOWERS

Clematis (*Clematis*) pp.118–119
Cobaea scandens pp.134–135
Sea hollies (*Eryngium*) pp.68–69

Geraniums (*Geranium*) pp.120–121
Morning glory (*Ipomoea*) pp.134–135
Sweet peas (*Lathyrus odoratus*) pp.56–57

QUICK FIX, *above*
In no time at all, *Crambe cordifolia* produces statuesque mounds, ideal for gaps at the back of the flower border.

FAST WORKER, *left*
The vigorous *Prunella grandiflora* soon covers the ground and by summer is topped with clusters of rich purple flowers.

PLANT	SIZE	APPEARANCE
CANNAS *Canna* Z 8–11	H 24–32in (60–80cm) S 18in (45cm)	The combination of large, flamboyant leaves and trumpet-shaped flowers in brilliant shades of red, orange, or yello‍ make cannas real attention-grabbers. T flower from midsummer-on.
SPIDER FLOWER *Cleome hassleriana* Annual	H 4ft (1.2m) S 18in (45cm)	This annual produces striking, spidery, pink, white, or purple, strongly scente‍ flowers in dense clusters held on tower‍ stems. They are borne from early summer until frost.
CRAMBE *Crambe cordifolia* Z 6–9	H 8ft (2.4m) S 5ft (1.5m)	This superb, unusually large, mound-forming perennial is covered with mas‍ of tiny, star-shaped white flowers in ea‍ summer, creating a pretty, cloudlike h‍ with a sweet perfume.
TWINSPURS *Diascia* Z 7–9	H 18in (45cm) S 16in (40cm)	These perennials bear large numbers o‍ delicate pink, peachy, or near-red flow‍ in loose spikes throughout the summe‍ and into early autumn. They are not reliably hardy and prefer cool weather.
PERENNIAL PEA *Lathyrus latifolius* Z 5–9	H 10ft (3m) S 3ft (90cm)	A very fast-growing and vigorous herbaceous climber that soon clamber‍ a trellis or through shrubs. Flowers are scented but come in white or lovely sh‍ of pink or red in summer to early autu‍
PURPLE LOOSESTRIFE *Lythrum salicaria* Z 4–9	H 4ft (1.2m) S 18in (45cm)	This is a real hit with butterflies and be‍ In midsummer plants are smothered ir‍ dense spikes of flowers in shades of pin‍ *L. salicaria* and its varieties reliably bring‍ splashes of color to borders.
SOLOMON'S SEAL *Polygonatum odoratum* Z 4–8	H 2ft (60cm) S 12in (30cm)	Any shady spot can be given a quick lif‍ spring by this fragrant perennial. The foliage is pretty, and the scented white flowers, tinged with green, hang from delicately arching stems.
SELFHEAL *Prunella grandiflora* Z 5–8	H 10in (25cm) S 3ft (90cm)	Useful as a groundcover, this perennial produces violet, purple, white, or pink flowers throughout the summer. The flowers develop on small spikes within ring of showy, leafy bracts.
Sisyrinchium striatum Z 7–8	H 18–24in (45–60cm) S 12in (30cm)	The sword-shaped leaves of this perenn‍ striped in the bold variety 'Variegatum' held in a distinct fan. Cream or yellowis‍ flowers, held in dense spikes, appear throughout the summer.
SPIDERWORTS *Tradescantia* Z 5–9	H 16–24in (45–60cm) S 18in (45cm)	A pretty, clump-forming perennial that produces a succession of three-petaled flowers from early summer to early autumn. Depending on the variety, flo‍ color is blue, purple, pink, or white.

SITE	CULTIVATION	HINTS AND TIPS
Cannas need fertile soil and plenty of sun and water.	Plant in spring, after the last frosts are over. In autumn, lift the fleshy roots, remove dead areas, and store in sawdust in a cool, frost-free place.	• In early spring, plant stored roots in individual pots of soil mix and sand. Keep in a warm greenhouse until it is time to plant them. • My favorites are 'Wyoming', 'Black Knight', 'Rosemond Coles', 'Pretoria' and 'Durban'.
Likes well-drained soil in sun.	Sow spider flower seed in a warm greenhouse in mid-spring. Plant out as soon as the last frosts are over in late spring or early summer.	• Transplant when small to avoid root disturbance, which produces shorter plants, or sow direct. • Striking varieties include 'Helen Campbell', 'Violet Queen', 'Pink Queen' and 'Cherry Queen'. • Spider flowers thrive in large containers.
Prefers a sunny site with well-drained soil. Will thrive in poor soil.	Plant in autumn or early spring. Divide established plants in late spring. Sow seed in spring in a warm greenhouse, pot up, then plant out when large enough.	• Crambe is an ideal plant for the back of the border, providing a good textural backdrop for all sorts of color combinations. • Crambe dies back shortly after flowering, so plant the gap left with annuals.
Well-drained but moist soil in sun or part shade.	Best planted in spring, adding a balanced fertilizer to the soil. Divide established plants in spring or take semiripe cuttings in summer.	• After the first flush of flowers, cut the plants back; a second, later display might develop. • Lovely varieties include 'Lilac Belle', 'Rupert Lambert', 'Salmon Supreme', 'Blackthorn Apricot', and 'Ruby Field'.
Thrives in any reasonable soil in sun or part shade.	Plant in spring and grow as a groundcover or as a climber. Seed can be sown direct into the ground in early spring or in individual pots.	• Cut flowers or deadhead regularly to prevent seeds from forming and so prolong flowering. • Slugs can be a problem, especially if the plants are grown as a groundcover. • For purplish pink flowers, choose the species.
Moist or even wet soil, in sun or part shade. Do not plant near wetlands.	Plant during suitable weather in autumn or spring. Divide established clumps in autumn or spring or take semiripe cuttings in spring.	• Deadhead regularly to encourage flowering and prevent self-sown seedlings. • Choose named varieties for the best-looking plants. I like 'Firecandle' (rose-pink), 'The Beacon' (even richer pink) and 'Robert' (bright pink).
Well-drained soil in dappled shade.	Plant during suitable conditions in late autumn or early spring, adding leafmold or compost to the soil. Divide established clumps in spring.	• If plants start to lose their vigor, lift and divide them, discarding the older sections. • May be attacked by deer. • For interesting foliage, try *P. odoratum* var. *pluriflorum* 'Variegatum'.
Either a sunny or partly shaded site. Selfheal grows well in almost all soils.	Best planted in early spring, self-heal is easy to grow and soon spreads to create a wonderful groundcover. Divide overgrown clumps in spring or autumn.	• Selfheal thrives on fairly poor soils, so don't overfeed or grow on a rich soil. • Among my favorites are *P. grandiflora* itself (violet), 'Loveliness' (lilac), 'Pink Loveliness', 'White Loveliness', and 'Rotkäppchen' (deep carmine).
Well-drained soil (especially in winter), in plenty of sun.	Best planted in spring – it needs regular watering to establish well, but cold and moisture together make it rot. Divide large clumps in spring.	• Set plants slightly above ground level to prevent water from puddling around the base. • Once established, sisyrinchiums have a tendency to self-seed, producing offspring in such quantity that they may become a nuisance.
Best in fertile soil in a sunny position.	An extremely easy plant to grow, spiderwort is best planted during spring or autumn. Divide established clumps in autumn or spring.	• Most of the named varieties are more compact than the species. I particularly like *T.* × *andersoniana* 'Isis' (light blue), 'Zwanenburg Blue' (pinkish lilac), and 'Carmine Glow' (carmine), and *T. virginiana* 'Caerulea Plena' (double, deep blue flowers).

SUMMER MAGIC
The sword-shaped leaves of *Sisyrinchium striatum* are often mistaken for those of iris, but the wands of delicate flowers are quite different.

TALL STORY
With a common name like spider flower, the strange but very striking appearance of *Cleome* in bloom comes as no surprise. Very useful for height in summer bedding.

MASS PRODUCTION
The loose flower spikes of *Diascia barberae* 'Blackthorn Apricot' are so plentiful that they create a wonderful mound of color.

Flowering climbers

WITHOUT HEIGHT, even an otherwise interesting garden can seem dull. By clothing arches, arbors, trellises, walls, and fences with climbing plants, any plot, large or small, becomes more exciting. Careful positioning also allows you to hide ugly features in or beyond the garden.

OTHER FLOWERING CLIMBERS

BOLD AND BRIGHT
Provided host plants are sturdy and won't be swamped, let climbers scramble over them for stunning combinations, such as this *Tropaeolum speciosum* in a dark yew.

Stamens and ovary have an elaborate and unusual structure

Exotic bowl-shaped flowers

A SPECIAL PASSION
Even from a distance the striking flowers of *Passiflora caerulea* have considerable impact, but a closer look reveals just how extraordinary they are.

PLANT	SIZE	APPEARANCE
TRUMPET VINE *Campsis radicans* Z 5–9	H 30ft (9m) S 3ft (90cm)	Clusters of gorgeous, bright orange-red yellow trumpet-shaped flowers, each u 3in (7.5cm) long, bloom during late summer and early autumn. Trumpet vi attract hummingbirds.
CUP-AND-SAUCER VINE *Cobaea scandens* Annual	H 10ft (3m) S 5ft (1.5m)	In just a single season this fast-growing produces many extraordinary, cup-sha fragrant flowers from midsummer unt the first frosts, so this tender perennial usually grown as an annual.
CHILEAN GLORY VINE *Eccremocarpus scaber* Z 10–11	H 10ft (3m) S 3ft (90cm)	This fabulously exotic climber is covere bunches of almost tubular orange flowe with yellow lips throughout the summ and into autumn. It is fast growing and its tendrils to cling to supports.
MORNING GLORY *Ipomoea* Annual	H 8–13ft (2.5–4m) S 3ft (90cm)	Large numbers of cheerful, trumpet-sha flowers in pink, red, blue, purple, or w appear from summer until early autumn Morning glory is fast-growing: grow fr seed each year as an annual.
SUMMER JASMINE *Jasminum officinale* Z 9–10	H 27ft (8m) S 10ft (3m)	If you like scent in the garden, you can without a jasmine! From midsummer early autumn this slow-growing, decid climber is covered in starry, trumpet-shaped, exquisitely perfumed white flo
HONEYSUCKLE *Lonicera* Z 4–10	H 5–13ft (1.5–4m) S 5–8ft (1.5–2.4m)	There are many good species and varie of these tough, woody perennial climb with their delicate yet elaborate, fragra flowers. Some flower as early as late sp others bloom into early autumn.
PASSIONFLOWER *Passiflora* Z 6–11	H 33ft (10m) S 4ft (1.2m)	Nothing can quite prepare you for the strange beauty of passionflowers – whi pink, or purple-tinged, with an intrica central display, borne from midsumme early autumn.
CHILEAN POTATO VINE *Solanum crispum* Z 9–10	H 13ft (4m) S 3ft (90cm)	This pretty scrambling plant produces numerous star-shaped, delicately fragr purple flowers with yellow stamens fro midsummer until early autumn. It is h only in mild areas.
FLAME CREEPER *Tropaeolum speciosum* Z 8–10	H 10ft (3m) S 2ft (60cm)	An attractive perennial climber, covere long-spurred, trumpet-shaped flame-r flowers from mid- to late summer. The flowers may be followed by bright blue berries in autumn.
Tropaeolum tuberosum Z 8–10	H 10ft (3m) S 2ft (60cm)	This fast-growing perennial climber produces elongated, bright orange-red flowers, each up to 1⅝in (4cm) long, fro midsummer until early autumn. The fo is prettily lobed and gray-green.

SITE	CULTIVATION	HINTS AND TIPS
A sunny spot and moist, free-draining soil.	Ideally, plant at the end of summer or in early spring and feed and water regularly. Provide a support, such as a wall, to which the creeper can cling.	• Choose a sunny wall or trellis in a quiet spot to attract hummingbirds. • Trumpet vines are strong and fast-growing; make sure the support you choose is capable of withstanding the weight.
Plant in well-drained soil in a sunny spot sheltered from wind.	Plant in early summer and provide netting or wires for it to scramble up. Rapid growth makes it a hungry feeder, and plenty of water is important.	• Raise from seed sown in individual pots in a warm greenhouse in early spring. • The flowers open creamy green and age to purple. The variety 'Alba' has white flowers turning to cream.
Requires a sunny spot and well-drained soil.	Best planted in spring and treated as an annual. If you provide winter protection where marginally hardy, it may regrow in the spring.	• The Chilean glory vine is a rampant self-seeder, so its tenderness is rarely a problem where marginally hardy because many seedlings usually appear in spring and grow rapidly. • Anglia hybrids come in a range of flower colors.
A sunny spot with any reasonable soil.	Sow seed in early to midspring and plant out as soon as all frosts are over, or sow direct. They need support from wires, a trellis, or other plants.	• Grown in dappled shade, flowering is reduced, but you still get a pretty show. • Soak seeds in water overnight before sowing to speed up germination and increase success. • *I. tricolor* 'Heavenly Blue' has the best blue flowers.
A well-drained soil is best, in sun or part shade.	Plant in spring or summer. It twines, so needs a support of thin wires or slats, such as a trellis or other framework. Take semi-ripe cuttings in summer.	• Don't panic about its ultimate size; jasmine takes about five years before it reaches 12ft (3.5m). • For delightfully variegated foliage that gives the whole plant a shimmering, silvery look, choose the variety 'Argenteovariegatum'.
Not fussy; avoid poorly draining or overly dry soil. Sun or dappled shade.	Ideally, plant honeysuckle in spring or autumn, if possible with the roots in the shade. Water and feed regularly in spring and early summer.	• Fantastic climbers for a pergola or arbor where you can easily enjoy the fragrance. • Routine pruning is not necessary, but thin out straggly plants and reduce large ones by pruning in spring, or in autumn in warm areas.
Choose a spot with well-drained soil in full sun.	Best planted in spring near a wall in all-day or afternoon sun in a sheltered position. It will require supports to clamber on.	• Protect in winter in the first few years and during harsh winters. If the stems are killed by frost, the plant almost always reshoots from the base. • After flowering, the plant may produce yellow-orange or green fruits.
Needs a very sheltered spot with plenty of sun and well-drained soil.	Preferably plant in spring; add extra sand to the planting hole to encourage good drainage in all but the best-drained soils. Water frequently during summer.	• You must provide a trellis or system of wires to which the plant can attach itself. • For protection, try a winter "blanket" of dry leaves or straw held in place with chicken wire. • For deep purple-blue flowers choose 'Glasnevin'.
A sunny position with well-drained but moist soil.	Plant in spring. Keep the roots moist during summer. The roots spread to make new plants; divide in early spring, or sow seed under glass in spring.	• Flame creepers need a framework over which they can scramble. Use them to brighten up existing shrubs or climbers, or along hedges; because the roots run along under the ground, plants pop up in different places each year.
Plant in well-drained yet moist soil, in plenty of sun.	Lift the tubers in early winter and store them in dry compost or sawdust in a cool but frost-free place. Separate tubers in early autumn.	• One of the quickest ways of covering bare trellis with flowers, perhaps while slower-growing plants mature. • Slugs like to eat young growth, so if necessary take precautions, particularly early in the season.

EARLY VISITOR
Why not grow morning glory (here, *Ipomoea tricolor*) to create a quick wall of color while longer-lasting woody climbers get established?

SWEET SIMPLICITY
The simple white flowers of *Jasminum officinale* 'Argenteovariegatum' help lighten a slightly shady spot, especially with its variegated foliage.

POWERFUL BEAUTY
The deeply fragrant Japanese honeysuckle (*Lonicera japonica*) grows very vigorously.

Easy annuals

CHOOSE ANY OF THE plants here, and you can sow them directly into your garden soil without having to bother with seed trays or soil mix. Sow at intervals in spring (with some you can start the previous autumn), and they'll put on a superb show all through the summer.

OTHER ANNUALS TO SOW DIRECT

Baby's breath (*Gypsophila*) pp.150—151
Sunflowers (*Helianthus*) pp.82—83
Morning glory (*Ipomoea*) pp.134—135
Sweet peas (*Lathyrus odoratus*) pp.56—57
Poppies (*Papaver*) pp.110—111
Scabiosa (*Scabiosa*) pp.150—151

DAY OF THE TRIFFIDS
Who says triffids are ugly or frightening? The beautiful pink-purple flowers of *Malope trifida* more than make up for its Latin name!

HISTORY LESSON
The dazzlingly bright flowers of pot marigolds are always a welcome sight and have been popular in the garden for centuries — they are often featured in reconstructed Colonial kitchen and herb gardens.

PLANT	SIZE	APPEARANCE
POT MARIGOLDS *Calendula officinalis*	H 8in (20cm) S 12in (30cm)	Favorites with children, pot marigolds orange, cream, or yellow daisy- or pomponlike flowers for most of the summer. The foliage is strongly aroma said by some to deter cats!
CANDYTUFT *Iberis amara*	H 10in (25cm) S 6in (15cm)	With its slightly fragrant, dome-shape heads of small, white, lilac, or pink flo candytuft is a magnet for butterflies ar beneficial insects such as syrphid flies. annual blooms throughout the summ
ANNUAL MALLOW *Lavatera trimestris*	H 2—3ft (60—90cm) S 18in (45m)	Choose mallow if you want a plant tha instantly looks as if it's been there fore This sturdy, bushy annual is covered ir flowers up to 4in (10cm) across from midsummer to early autumn.
POACHED-EGG PLANT *Limnanthes douglasii*	H 6in (15cm) S 6in (15cm)	This plant's common name perfectly describes its flowers, with bright egg-yo yellow centers surrounded by white pe Bees love it, and it brings a splash of col from late spring until the end of summ
FLAX *Linum grandiflorum*	H 12—18in (30—45cm) S 3in (7.5cm)	Large numbers of small, saucer-shaped pale pink flowers are produced by the plant from mid- to late summer. The s and foliage of this annual are a lovely, complementary delicate green.
VIRGINIA STOCK *Malcolmia maritima*	H 10in (20cm) S 12in (30cm)	These are some of the simplest and qu annuals to grow, often flowering just o month after spring sowing to form de clouds of scented flowers in shades of red, white, green, or purple.
MALOPE *Malope trifida*	H 3ft (90cm) S 12in (30cm)	If you enjoy cutting flowers to take ind make room for malope in your border large pink-purple flowers, marked wit purple veins, are in plentiful supply fro midsummer to midautumn.
NIGHT-SCENTED STOCK *Matthiola bicornis*	H 12in (30cm) S 10in (25cm)	Not as showy as other commonly grow stocks, but wait until dusk and you'll b over by its intense, sweet perfume. Thi annual produces spikes of lilac flowers mid- to late summer.
BABY BLUE-EYES *Nemophila menziesii*	H 18in (45cm) S 12in (30cm)	A quaint name for a pretty plant, baby eyes produces a mass of sky blue flowe with white centers throughout summe until autumn — it's one of the longest- flowering annuals.
MIGNONETTE *Reseda odorata*	H 12—24in (30—60cm) S 6in (15cm)	This has a sensational fragrance, from spikes of minute greenish yellow or pa brown flowers. An annual loved by butterflies, it will grace your border fro midsummer until early autumn.

SITE	CULTIVATION	HINTS AND TIPS
Plant in well-drained soil, in full sun. Ideal for containers.	Sow in early to midspring; thin seedlings to 18–24in (45–60cm) apart. Sow at one- or two-week intervals to ensure a longer flowering period.	• Pot marigolds do not flower well if over-watered, or during hot, humid weather. Avoid later sowings if you expect these conditions. • I particularly like 'Radio Extra Selected', with its bright orange blooms, and 'Apricot Pygmy'.
Well-drained soil, in a sunny position.	Best sown direct in early or midspring (they dislike being sown in seed trays). Candytuft performs better than most annuals in a dry situation.	• Sow in drifts or clumps between larger plants. • 'Dwarf Fairyland Mixed' produces plants 8–10in (20–25cm) tall, with a mixture of maroon, carmine, lilac, and white flowers. • Collect the seedheads to use dried.
Excellent for a dry, sunny site – against a sunny wall, perhaps.	Sow seed in early to midspring; thin seedlings to 18in (45cm) apart. Water young plants regularly; established plants are fairly drought tolerant.	• Keep an eye out for aphids, which often attack tender young growth. • My favorite varieties are 'Silver Cup', with bright pink flowers, the pure white 'Mont Blanc', and the cerise-pink 'Ruby Regis'.
Moisture-retentive soil, in sun.	Sow seed in early spring or the previous autumn and thin out to about 6in (15cm) apart. Keep seedlings and plants well watered. Will self-seed.	• Very easily grown and quick to flower: a great gap-filler in a perennial border. • Good as border edging or on a rocky area. • Plant close to roses – the larvae of the syrphid flies they attract will devour aphids.
Choose a sunny spot with well-drained soil.	Best sown early spring or early the previous autumn. Thin seedlings to about 5in (13cm) apart, close enough to grow into each other but not cramped.	• Linum grandiflorum 'Album' has pure white flowers (1½in/4cm wide), readily producing them in loose clusters. • For something more fiery, L. rubrum has beautiful, satiny red flowers with dark centers.
Any site with well-drained soil, in plenty of sun.	Sown in spring, these stocks will usually flower just a few weeks later. Seed can also be sown in autumn for flowers the next summer.	• Sow batches of seed every two weeks or so to enjoy the flowers and fragrance of Virginia stocks throughout the summer. • Drizzle seed into soil-filled gaps between paving for splashes of cottage garden-style color.
Any soil will do, but make sure that malopes get plenty of sun.	Sow in midspring and thin seedlings to about 12in (30cm) apart. Prompt removal of faded flowers will increase the length of the flowering period.	• I love 'Pink Queen', with shell-pink flowers, and 'White Queen', with pure white flowers. Each grows to a stately 2–3ft (60–90cm). • For a lovely mixture of pink, white, red, and purple flowers, try 'Large Flowered Hybrids'.
A sunny or partly shaded spot with well-fertilized, moist soil.	Sow in late spring, in drifts or among other annuals or perennials. Thin seedlings to about 8–10in (20–25cm) apart. Keep well watered at all times.	• Position stocks close to open windows, arbors, or other areas where you may sit in the evening. • Add seeds to hanging baskets and other containers. For really showy pink flowers, look out for the variety 'Pink Scentsation'.
Moisture-retentive soil, in sun or part shade.	Sow in early to midspring and keep seedlings and plants well watered. I use twiggy sticks to support these plants, since they tend to flop.	• Baby blue-eyes are good in containers as well as in borders, but keep them well watered. • For contrast, 'Total Eclipse' is nearly black with a neat white edge to the petals; 'Pale Face' is white and covered in tiny black freckles.
Well-drained soil, in plenty of sun.	Sow in mid- to late spring; if the weather is still quite cool, apply a loose mulch to keep the soil warm. Thin seedlings to 12in (30cm) apart.	• Mignonette grows rapidly, so several planted together produce a really fast gap filler. • If you want a more showy plant, choose 'Fragrant Beauty', which has lime green flowers with a distinct red tinge.

SOFT TOUCH
The delicate-looking flowers of *Linum grandiflorum* 'Rubrum' belie its sturdy nature; it can be sown in autumn for early blooms.

HIGH AND DRY
Grown primarily for its perfume, *Reseda odorata* is perfect for a dry situation close to a patio or terrace.

CHOICE SELECTION
An annual relative of the shrubby lavatera, *Lavatera trimestris* 'Pink Beauty' is a lovely true pink.

Flowers for bees and butterflies

BEES AND BUTTERFLIES are a welcome sight in any garden, and by planting flowers that they find attractive, you can be sure that you will have plenty of these small visitors for as long as the plants are in bloom. The pollinating activity of the bees will also be welcome if you grow produce.

OTHER FLOWERS FOR BEES AND BUTTERFLIES

Perennial asters (*Aster*) pp.78–79
Foxgloves (*Digitalis*) pp.42–43
Sea hollies (*Eryngium*) pp.68–69
Sweet peas (*Lathyrus odoratus*) pp.56–57
Lavenders (*Lavandula*) pp.70–71
Sedum spectabile pp.156–157

PRETTY RICH, *left*
Butterflies love pinks and mauves – here *Origanum laevigatum* 'Herrenhausen' has attractively tinted foliage that adds to the rich mid-purple of the flowers.

MOONSTRUCK, *below*
This *Coreopsis* 'Moonbeam' looks as if it might blow away in a puff of wind, yet its stems will bear the weight of a bumblebee.

PLANT	SIZE		APPEARANCE
THRIFTS *Armeria* Z 5–8	H 2–4ft (60–120cm)	S 12–18in (30–45cm)	Who wouldn't be drawn to these deligh evergreen perennials? From the end of spring until midsummer they form mounds of pink or white, near-spheric flowerheads on long, straight stems.
PERENNIAL COREOPSIS *Coreopsis* Z 4–8	H 12–24in (30–60cm)	S 18in (45cm)	You can rely on coreopsis to produce a profusion of golden yellow flowers, eith single or double, for much of the summ and into early autumn. Although peren most will need replacing after a few yea
PERENNIAL GAILLARDIAS *Gaillardia* Z 3–8	H 10–30in (25–75cm)	S 18in (45cm)	Gaillardias bear startling, brightly colo daisylike flowers in red, orange, or yell often bicolored, for much of the summ and into early or midautumn, dependin on the variety.
AVENS *Geum chiloense* Z 5–9	H 10–30in (25–75cm)	S 10–20in (25–50cm)	The flowers of avens have such innocer open faces. Perennials, they bear bright orange, red, or yellow, single or double flowers with prominent, usually yellow stamens, throughout much of summer
ROCK ROSES *Helianthemum* Z 6–8	H 8–18in (20–45cm)	S 12–24in (30–60cm)	From late spring until early summer th shrubby evergreens are covered in beau open flowers with delicate petals in dazzling shades of red, orange, yellow, pink, or cream.
LIGULARIA *Ligularia dentata* Z 4–8	H 4–6ft (1.2–1.8m)	S 2ft (60cm)	Like golden beacons in the flower bord these imposing perennials have tall, compact spikes of tiny daisylike flowers shades of orange or yellow from the m to the end of summer.
BEE BALM *Monarda* Z 4–9	H 2–4ft (60–120cm)	S 12–18in (30–45cm)	Bees just can't get enough of these unu tufted flowers in white or shades of pin purple, mauve, or red. These fairly sho lived perennials or biennials bloom for much of the summer.
CATMINT *Nepeta* Z 3–9	H 12–36in (30–90cm)	S 24–30in (60–75cm)	Both cats and bees find most species of catmint irresistible. These superb low-growing perennials produce fragile-loo flower spikes in white or shades of purp or blue all through summer.
OREGANO *Origanum laevigatum* Z 7–10	H 20–24in (50–60cm)	S 18in (45cm)	The purple flowers may be tiny, but the are grouped together into impressive clusters from midsummer until mid-autumn. The foliage of this perennial is blue-green and aromatic.
POTENTILLA *Potentilla* Z 5–8	H 18in (45cm)	S 2ft (60cm)	These perennials produce masses of pre red, orange, yellow, or pink flowers, wh are either single or semidouble. They bloom throughout the summer, set of attractive, often silvery, foliage.

SITE	CULTIVATION	HINTS AND TIPS
Well-drained soil and plenty of sun.	Best planted in spring, thrifts pretty well look after themselves. Divide established plants in late summer or take semiripe cuttings in summer.	• Use thrifts to form neat, colorful edging to paths, borders, and steps. They are also at home in alpine troughs or rock gardens. Many thrifts are maritime plants, so they stand up well to buffeting by the wind.
Prefer a sunny spot with well-drained soil.	Plant in spring. Coreopsis benefit from being fed with a high-potassium fertilizer to ensure plenty of flowers. Support taller plants. Deadhead regularly.	• Annual coreopsis are also available. • Young plants are easily raised from seed sown in a propagating case in early spring. • For softer color schemes, the single flowers of *C. rosea* are a lovely pale pink.
Anywhere with well-drained soil and plenty of sun.	Ideally, sow the seed direct into spare ground in spring, grow on, and transfer into their flowering sites the following spring. Divide established plants in spring.	• Taller plants may need supports. • Gaillardias need good drainage to overwinter; even then, their lifespan is only about three years. • Annual gaillardias can be raised from seed sown direct in late spring or early summer.
Need soil that retains moisture but is well drained, ideally in full sun.	Planted in spring or autumn, they are easy to look after. Deadhead regularly to prolong flowering. Divide established plants in autumn or early spring.	• Avens will perform surprisingly well in part or dappled shade, but flowering will be less showy and the plants are likely to become leggier. • For damp, shadier spots try *G. rivale* (water avens), which has pink or cream bell-like flowers.
Well-drained soil and plenty of sun are essential.	Plant in spring, and incorporate coarse sand if your soil is not extremely free-draining already. Take semiripe cuttings in mid- to late summer.	• Clip shortly after the flowers have faded to keep growth dense and bushy. • Choose a sheltered site to ensure the most prolific flowering and to prevent flowers and foliage from being spoiled by winds.
Choose a site in dappled shade, sheltered from sun and wind, with moist soil.	Plant in autumn or spring. Incorporate coarse organic matter to improve soil moisture retention. Divide established plants in autumn or spring.	• Tall plants will need support. • Ligularia thrive growing close to ponds as well as in moist borders. • Try 'Othello' for its purplish leaves; 'Desdemona' has brown-green leaves with red-brown undersides.
They need fairly moist soil in either sun or part shade.	Best planted in spring or autumn. If your soil has a tendency to dry out, add coarse organic matter, which will hold moisture before planting.	• After three or four years bee balms start to decline and are best replaced with fresh plants. • For the most startlingly bright red flowers, choose 'Cambridge Scarlet'. • Divide established plants in spring.
Choose a well-drained site with plenty of sun.	These easy plants are best planted in spring. Deadheading improves flowering. Divide mature plants in early spring, or take softwood cuttings at the end of spring.	• 'Six Hills Giant' is covered in delicate lavender-colored flower spikes throughout the summer. • As their common name suggests, cats are frequently attracted to these plants – especially *N. cataria* – and enjoy lying or rolling on them!
Well-drained soil and full sun are essential.	Ideally, plant in spring. Incorporate sand to improve drainage if necessary. Divide established clumps, or take softwood cuttings in spring.	• For lots of new plants in spring, sow seeds in a propagating case in autumn. • Since *O. laevigatum* is also a useful culinary herb (often used to flavor Italian dishes), you might want to plant some close to the house.
Need a reasonably well-drained soil and plenty of sun.	Best planted in spring or autumn, potentillas soon form impressive clumps. Divide established plants in early spring.	• Cut off flower stems as soon as the flowers have faded; this can prolong flowering into autumn. • For warm shades, I love 'Gibson's Scarlet' (bright scarlet), 'William Rollison' (semidouble reddish orange) and 'Melton' (reddish pink).

BRIGHT AND BEAUTIFUL
Although less than knee high, the bright flowers of *Gaillardia × grandiflora* 'Kobold' more than compensate for its size.

SUMMER SENSATION
The large, lavender-colored flowers of *Nepeta sibirica* are loosely packed on upright stems to stunning effect on this rather tall catmint.

LEADING LIGHT
Insects are attracted to flat, single flowers; with its dark-centered, almost luminously bright blooms, *Potentilla* 'Gibson's Scarlet' would be hard to miss.

Flowers for dry places

WATER SHORTAGES can have a devastating effect on gardens, but if you grow plants that prefer dry conditions you can still have great-looking borders. The plants here will also thrive in soil that is light and sandy, and love full sun: perfect for hot, dry gardens.

OTHER FLOWERS FOR DRY PLACES

Rock roses (*Cistus*) pp.112–113
Sunflowers (*Helianthus*) pp.82–83
Red-hot pokers (*Kniphofia*) pp.38–39
Lavender (*Lavandula*) pp.70–71
Osteospermums (*Osteospermum*) pp.86–87
Thymes (*Thymus*) pp.130–131

SOME LIKE IT HOT, *right*
Introduce the fiery colors of zinnias into a really hot spot. Here, the flowers of *Zinnia haageana* 'Persian Carpet' are like glowing embers.

TOUSLED CHARMER, *left*
The shaggy, bright pink flower spikes of *Liatris spicata* remind me of a bad hair day! They look marvelous among plants with bronze or purple foliage.

PLANT	SIZE	APPEARANCE
CERATOSTIGMA *Ceratostigma plumbaginoides* Z 6–9	H 18in (45cm) S 2ft (60cm)	Startlingly bright blue flowers burst ou over this shrubby perennial from late summer until the middle of autumn. bonus, the deciduous foliage turns brig red in autumn.
SILVER BUSH *Convolvulus cneorum* Z 8–10	H 2ft (60cm) S 2ft (60cm)	This rounded, shrubby plant is usually covered with white funnel-shaped flow from late spring through the end of summer. The downy foliage is an exqu silvery color.
FLANNEL BUSH *Fremontodendron* Z 8–10	H 16ft (5m) S 6ft 6in (2m)	The showy, bright yellow flowers of th wall shrub crowd the stems for much the summer. The leaves are covered in minute bristly hairs and, in mild areas, semievergreen.
GAZANIAS *Gazania* Z 8–10	H 6–12in (15–30cm) S 6–12in (15–30cm)	These perennials won't survive winter but can easily be grown as annuals. Mo bear daisylike flowers in shades of oran yellow, red, or brown from early summ to midautumn.
LEWISIAS *Lewisia* Z 4–8	H 12in (30cm) S 12in (30cm)	From late spring to the end of summer these fleshy-leaved perennials produce good supply of vividly colored, cheerfu flowers in bright shades of orange, pink purple, yellow, or cream.
GAYFEATHERS *Liatris* Z 4–9	H 2–3ft (60–90cm) S 30cm (12in)	The pink, white, or purple flower spike gayfeathers look rather like shaggy bot brushes. In flower throughout the summer, these hardy perennials are als favorite with butterflies.
ROSE CAMPION *Lychnis coronaria* Z 4–8	H 2ft (60cm) S 18in (45cm)	The silvery, furry foliage makes a lovel backdrop for the bright flowers in whit shades of pink or reddish purple that appear in summer. This perennial is popular with butterflies.
Tithonia rotundifolia Annual	H 4–10ft (1.2–3m) S 20–36in (50–90cm)	Although Mexican sunflower is less oft grown than traditional *Helianthus* it can the latter a run for its money, producin delicately scented, bright orange flowers from midsummer to midautumn.
YUCCAS *Yucca* Z 5–10	H 2–3ft (60–90cm) S 30–36in (75–90cm)	Even when not in flower, you can't mis these dramatic plants with their spiky rosettes of swordlike leaves. The cream colored flower spikes rise up to 5–6ft (1.5–1.8m) in mid- to late summer.
ZINNIAS *Zinnia* Annual	H 16–24in (40–60cm) S 12in (30cm)	These dahlialike flowers have an unabas exuberance and come in orange, yellow reddish purple, pink, or white, flowerin from midsummer to midautumn. The grown as annuals.

TE	CULTIVATION	HINTS AND TIPS
warm, dry te with well-rained soil.	Best planted in spring or autumn. If given the protection of a south- or west-facing wall it will perform to its peak. Divide large plants during spring.	• Quite late to emerge in spring, so mark the site or grow among spring-flowering bulbs to prevent accidental damage. • Take semiripe cuttings at the end of summer to make new plants.
free-draining oil and plenty f sun are ssential.	Ideally, plant in spring, adding sand unless the soil is very well drained. Take semiripe cuttings with a heel in summer; overwinter in a greenhouse.	• A sheltered site, perhaps close to a wall, is ideal; it provides winter protection. • This lovely plant is readily killed or reduced to a straggly mess by wet conditions over winter. Improve drainage or grow in a well-drained pot.
ell-drained oil in full sun, referably with he protection f a warm wall.	Best planted in autumn or spring. No need for routine pruning, but where shoots stick out from the wall, prune back after the main flush of flowers is over.	• Protect with loose leaves or straw held in place with chicken wire. • The hairy stems can cause skin and eye irritation, so wear gloves and goggles when pruning. • Thrives in alkaline soil.
enty of sun nd good rainage are ssential.	Sow seed in a propagating case in early spring. Harden off, then plant out in late spring or early summer when there is no risk of late frost. Deadhead regularly.	• Gazanias can be kept over winter if you have a greenhouse; lift and pot up in autumn. • Will not flower well in heavily fertilized or recently manured soil. • For a strong display try 'Daybreak Bright Orange'.
ery well-rained acidic neutral soil is ssential, ideally part shade.	Plant in spring, incorporating coarse sand to improve drainage. Increase stocks by carefully removing plantlets or dividing the plants in spring.	• Plant slightly shallowly and then surround with a layer of gravel to ensure that excess water does not accumulate around their crowns. • They look great grown in crevices in walls, in rock gardens, or on well-drained banks beside steps.
or best results, eeds a site ith well-rained soil and enty of sun.	Best planted in spring; add sand to improve drainage on heavier soils. Remove faded flower spikes regularly. Divide established clumps in spring.	• Like many other plants here, they can be grown in part shade, but flowering will be reduced. • For bright white flower spikes choose 'Floristan Weiss', for bright lilac-pink grow 'Kobold', and for purple go for 'Floristan Violett'.
ell-drained oil, in sun or ppled shade.	Best planted in spring; autumn planting should also be successful if the soil is very well drained. Sow seed in a propagating case in late winter.	• Rose campion is often rather short-lived but may be treated as an annual. Seeds started early will flower in their first year. • I particularly like the Alba Group (white) and 'Angel's Blush' (white with a pink flush).
elect a heltered site ith well-rained soil and enty of sun.	Sow seed in early spring, prick out into individual pots, harden off, then plant out when the last frosts are over. Taller varieties may need supporting.	• Regular removal of fading flowers prolongs the flowering period. • I like 'Torch', which has vibrant red flowers; for a smaller plant with deep orange flowers and yellow centers, go for 'Goldfinger'.
ll sun, and il with good rainage.	Best planted in spring; add sand to improve drainage if necessary. On mature plants, remove suckers with root systems at their bases in spring and plant.	• Occasionally leaves may be spoiled by fungal leaf spot infections; prune these out or treat with a suitable fungicide. • These drought-tolerant plants are good for pots and will survive summer neglect.
ell-drained oil and plenty sun.	Sow in early spring in a propagating case. After hardening off, plant out when the last of the frosts are over, or sow in late spring directly into the soil.	• Once growing, zinnias actually prefer not to be watered again. • Regular deadheading prolongs flowering. • Flowering is often disappointing in cool summers – these plants really love a hot, dry spot!

SUN LOVERS
Not for the faint-hearted, these *Gazania* Chansonette Series offer brightly colored, starry flowers that seem to soak up the sun.

SMALL SUCCESSES
Many of the smaller drought-tolerant plants, such as this *Lewisia*, may thrive where little else will grow.

GOOD SHOW
Growing flowering climbers against a very sunny, dry wall can be extremely difficult, but *Fremontodendron* – here 'Pacific Sunset' – provides a colorful and successful solution to the problem.

Flowers for damp places

FACED WITH AN AREA of boggy or wet ground, especially in shade, it's easy to be put off. If there is one secret to gardening, it is to work with rather than against the site, so choose plants that will positively thrive in this environment, and you can be sure of a beautiful display.

OTHER FLOWERS FOR DAMP PLACES

Montbretias (*Crocosmia*) pp.156–157	Hostas (*Hosta*) pp.158–159
Bleeding hearts (*Dicentra*) pp.98–99	*Lythrum salicaria* pp.132–133
Daylilies (*Hemerocallis*) pp.156–157	*Tiarella cordifolia* pp.160–161

BIG AND BOLD, *right*
There are lots of different species and varieties of filipendula for damp areas, all with interesting foliage topped by unruly flowerheads. Here, *Filipendula purpurea* is used as a groundcover.

WATER BABIES, *below*
In any moist soil astilbes can be guaranteed to produce a mass of foliage and extraordinary flowers. Here, *Astilbe chinensis* var. *taquetii* 'Purpurlanze' blooms in pink-purple.

PLANT	SIZE	APPEARANCE
ASTILBE *Astilbe* Z 4–8	H 12–24in (30–60cm) S 16–36in (40–90cm)	Similar in shape to ostrich plumes, fea[...] spikes of tiny flowers in white, red, and [...] shades appear throughout the summer[...] perennial has many good named varie[...] all with attractive, divided foliage.
MARSH MARIGOLD *Caltha palustris* Z 3–7	H 16in (40cm) S 20in (50cm)	The golden yellow buttercup-like flow[...] of this perennial plant bring a glorious[...] splash of color into boggy areas in spri[...] The large, glossy, kidney-shaped leaves[...] an added bonus.
SHOOTING STARS *Dodecatheon* Z 4–8	H 18–24in (45–60cm) S 8–12in (20–30cm)	Unusual nodding flowers with swept-[...] petals and prominent stamens are carr[...] on tall spikes. These perennials flower[...] white, purple, magenta, or pink, from [...] to late spring.
MEADOWSWEET *Filipendula* Z 3–9	H 12–24in (30–60cm) S 12–18in (30–45cm)	These eye-catching perennials flower f[...] mid- to late summer. 'Kahome' is my[...] favorite for its combination of bright p[...] almost frothy-looking flowerheads and[...] attractive, bright green foliage.
YELLOW FLAG *Iris pseudacorus* Z 5–8	H 2–5ft (60–150cm) S 2–3ft (60–90cm)	Bold, bright yellow flowers are produc[...] toward the end of spring, surrounded [...] fans of sword-shaped leaves. If you can[...] grow yellow flag in shallow water, it sh[...] reach even greater heights.
CARDINAL FLOWER *Lobelia cardinalis* Z 3–9	H 2–3ft (60–90cm) S 8–10in (20–25cm)	This perennial lobelia will bowl you ov[...] with its showy spikes of bright scarlet[...] blooms, and it attracts hummingbirds [...] butterflies. A short-lived perennial, it [...] flowers in mid- to late summer.
SCARLET MONKEY FLOWER *Mimulus cardinalis* Z 6–9	H 3ft (90cm) S 2ft (60cm)	The common name suggests somethin[...] exotic and colorful, and this perennial [...] doesn't disappoint with its yellow-thro[...] dazzling orange-red flowers that bloo[...] throughout the summer.
Ranunculus aconitifolius 'Flore Pleno' Z 5–9	H 2ft (60cm) S 18in (45cm)	The white flowers of this hardy perenn[...] appear in great quantity from late sprin[...] until midsummer. In the double variet[...] 'Flore Pleno' they are so crowded with [...] petals that they resemble tiny pompons.
GLOBEFLOWERS *Trollius* × *cultorum* Z 5–8	H 3ft (90cm) S 2ft (60cm)	From late spring to early or midsumm[...] showy yellow or orange flowers brighte[...] any moist or slightly boggy site. The le[...] of these perennials resemble those of t[...] relatives, the buttercups.
CALLA LILY *Zantedeschia aethiopica* Z 8–10	H 30–36in (75–90cm) S 20–24in (50–60cm)	'Crowborough' is the star among calla[...] lilies, with its elegant white spathes [...] surrounding a thin yellow flower spike[...] flowers from midspring until early sum[...] and is a bit hardier than the species.

ITE	CULTIVATION	HINTS AND TIPS
ich, well- rtilized, moist oil is essential. art shade is est.	Plant in autumn or spring; spacing depends on the variety chosen. Water regularly if the soil is not naturally moist. Divide established plants in autumn.	• Don't remove the spikes once they are faded; they turn a rich, handsome brown for the autumn and winter. • Occasionally, late frosts spoil the flowers, so consider using fleece to protect them.
lust have noist or even oggy soil. hoose a sunny osition.	Plant in autumn or spring, watering in well in all but the wettest sites. If possible, plant so that the roots are shaded from the heat of the sun.	• You can divide established clumps in the autumn or as soon as flowering is over. • Marsh marigolds will perform beautifully standing in up to about 5in (12.5cm) of water, so plant them in your pond or pool, too.
moist but not aterlogged oot in full sun r dappled hade.	Plant in autumn or spring; if the soil is not very moisture- retentive, add plenty of coarse organic matter. A cool, partly shaded spot is best.	• Never allow the soil to dry out. • Slugs and snails may be a problem early in the year, so take precautions if necessary. • Divide established clumps in early spring or as soon as the flowers have faded.
leeds moist or ven boggy soil a sun or part hade.	Best planted in autumn or spring. Keep well watered, especially early on and if the soil shows any sign of drying out. Apply a mulch if growing in sun.	• For more unusual foliage, try F. ulmaria 'Aurea', which has golden leaves. It's also much larger, growing to 5ft (1.5m) tall. • Divide plants in midautumn or very early spring if you want to increase your stocks.
hrives in moist oil, or in water p to 18in (45cm) eep, in sun or art shade.	Ideally, plant in autumn or early spring. Provided it has enough water, it is easy to look after. Planting in pond baskets makes lifting and dividing easier.	• Divide every three or four years, since this helps keep the clumps vigorous and flowering well. • To keep yellow flags at a manageable size for small ponds, always use pond baskets; growing freely in water, they can become much too large.
equires moist o boggy soil in un or part hade.	Plant in spring. Add plenty of coarse organic matter and water well if the soil tends to dry out in summer. Divide established clumps in spring.	• Ideally, protect the crowns over winter with a deep mulch of bark chips or straw held in place with a dome of chicken wire. • Although very showy, the cardinal flower is fairly short-lived, even in ideal growing conditions.
loist, fertile oil, in sun or art shade. refers slightly cid soil.	Best planted in autumn or early spring; add coarse organic matter to the planting hole, and water and mulch well, especially during summer, until established.	• Divide established clumps in either autumn or early to midspring. • The flowers attract bees and other insects, too. • Check labels carefully – some types of monkey flower are much larger and potentially invasive.
leeds a boggy oil in sun or appled shade.	Ideally, plant in autumn or spring; add leafmold or well- rotted manure. Divide established clumps as soon as the flowers have faded.	• Regular deadheading should encourage more flowers to be produced. • During dry spells check that the soil is not drying out at all, and water if necessary. Consider mulching moist soil, too.
moist site, in un or part hade.	Best planted in early to mid- autumn. Keep the soil moist at all times and deadhead to ensure the flowering period is as long as possible.	• Divide established clumps in early to midautumn. • Although related to buttercups, globe flowers are not invasive. • My favorite varieties are 'Orange Princess' (deep orange) and 'Lemon Queen' (pale yellow).
loist or boggy oil, or even a hallow pond nargin, in sun r part shade.	Easiest to establish if planted in early spring. In moist soils plant about 4in (10cm) deep; if grown in water, plant in a pond basket in up to 6in (15cm) of water.	• Divide established clumps of rhizomes toward the end of summer. • Provide winter protection by deep mulching. • If grown in water, do not let it freeze over – or lift and store plants in baskets.

IN THE SWIM
Unlike most of its relatives, *Iris pseudacorus*
will thrive in damp or even wet conditions.

MONKEY BUSINESS
For a splash of screaming scarlet in a
damp spot, *Mimulus cardinalis* is a
perfect choice. For a less startling
effect, there are named varieties in
subtler yellow, cream, and orange.

FALLING STARS
The flowers of shooting
stars (*Dodecatheon*) really
do look like tiny
heavenly bodies
plunging toward
the ground.

Flowers for shade

HAVING ONCE gardened under an army of trees, I know how frustrating it can be to work in shady conditions. If you try to grow sun-loving plants they'll never perform as you want them to, but fortunately there are plenty of plants that will bring welcome splashes of color to shade.

OTHER FLOWERS FOR SHADE

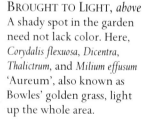

BROUGHT TO LIGHT, *above*
A shady spot in the garden need not lack color. Here, *Corydalis flexuosa*, *Dicentra*, *Thalictrum*, and *Milium effusum* 'Aureum', also known as Bowles' golden grass, light up the whole area.

FAME IS THE SPUR, *left*
There are blue, purplish red, and pink forms of *Corydalis flexuosa* from which to make your choice.

PLANT	SIZE	APPEARANCE
ELEPHANT'S EARS *Bergenia* Z 3–8	H 12–18in (30–45cm) S 12–18in (30–45cm)	It's not surprising these perennials are s widely grown – their evergreen foliage makes a good groundcover, they thriv shade, and they produce lots of spring flowers in white or shades of pink.
BUGBANES *Cimicifuga* Z 3–8	H 4–5ft (1.2–1.5m) S 2ft (60cm)	From late summer until midautumn, t tall perennials produce a plentiful sup elegant, often slightly arching spires, e made up of numerous tiny, white or c star-shaped flowers.
CORYDALIS *Corydalis solida,* *C. flexuosa* Z 5–8	H 8–12in (20–30cm) S 8–12in (20–30cm)	Dainty foliage is topped by clusters of equally delicate, spurred flowers from spring until early summer. These peren are naturally carpet-forming, with flo in shades of blue, pink, purple, or red.
LEOPARD'S BANE *Doronicum* Z 4–8	H 16–18in (40–45cm) S 16–24in (40–60cm)	Leopard's bane is amazingly versatile. will brighten a shady border in spring early summer, but you can grow this yellow-flowered daisylike perennial almost anywhere.
EPIMEDIUM *Epimedium* Z 5–9	H 8–16in (20–40cm) S 8–12in (20–30cm)	You couldn't ask for more graceful flo than these low-growing herbaceous or evergreen perennials. In spring, exquis spurred flowers appear in white or shades of pink, purple, yellow or red.
DOG'S-TOOTH VIOLETS *Erythronium* Z 3–9	H 6–12in (15–30cm) S 6–12in (15–30cm)	These nodding, trumpet-shaped flowe often with petals that curve backward, bring great elegance to the garden from mid- to late spring. These bulbs flower white, lilac, pink, or yellow.
MEADOWSWEET *Filipendula* Z 3–9	H 2–6ft (60–180cm) S 18–24in (45–60cm)	Tiny, fluffy flowers in white, pink, red, cream form such a mass of feathery plu that they look like clouds floating abov the plants. These perennials flower throughout the summer.
IMPATIENS *Impatiens* *walleriana* hybrids Annual	H 8–12in (20–30cm) S 8–12in (20–30cm)	Impatiens are almost always grown as annuals and raised or bought fresh eve year. They form dense mounds of flow pink, red, white, purple, or bicolored, f summer to frost.
TRILLIUMS *Trillium* Z 4–9	H 6–24in (15–60cm) S 4–18in (10–45cm)	Distinctive, three-petaled flowers are h singly above a set of three leaves. These choice perennials flower between midspring and very early summer in w pink, maroon, or greenish yellow.
WALDSTEINIA *Waldsteinia* *ternata* Z 3–9	H 6in (15cm) S 18in (45cm)	Diminutive saucer-shaped flowers in b yellow carpet the ground in profusion early summer. The flowers of this charming evergreen perennial have prominent masses of golden stamens.

ITE	CULTIVATION	HINTS AND TIPS
lephant's ears re not too ussy about soil, ut they prefer emishade.	Ideally, plant in autumn or spring. Although suited to semi-shade, stronger foliage color develops in sun. Divide mature clumps in spring or autumn.	• Many interesting species are available but generally flower less profusely than named hybrids. • For interesting autumn foliage, try 'Bressingham Ruby' (turns from green to maroon with crimson undersides) or *B. purpurascens* (flushes purple).
Choose a artially shaded pot with a noist, ideally cidic, soil.	Best planted in autumn or spring, preferably in a sheltered spot. In more exposed sites or if growing taller types, supports may be necessary.	• Divide established clumps in spring or autumn. • You can grow bugbanes in full sun, but there is a danger that the leaves may become scorched. • In dry weather, ensure that plants are kept moist at the roots. Mulching will help, too.
art shade with vell-drained oil full of rganic matter ideal.	Preferably plant in autumn or spring. Add plenty of well-rotted organic matter to improve soil texture. Keep well watered during dry weather.	• The best way to get new specimens is to divide established plants in spring or autumn. • Also try *C. lutea*, which has yellow flowers throughout summer, and *C. flexuosa* 'Purple Leaf', which has a purple tinge to its foliage.
Not fussy – will row in most easonable soils n shade, part hade, or sun.	Ideally, plant in early spring or autumn. After a few years the plants lose vigor, so regular division is advisable in late spring or early winter.	• Thrives on alkaline soils. • Deadhead regularly for a longer flowering period. • The deeper the shade, the taller the plant and the greater the likelihood that you will need to use twiggy sticks to support it.
Choose a well-rained yet umus-rich soil n partial shade r full sun.	Best planted in early spring or autumn, incorporating leafmold if necessary. Divide established plants in early spring or autumn.	• While the plants are establishing, keep them well watered and they will soon grow and spread. • Excellent for groundcover in the dappled shade beneath shrubs. As an added bonus, the foliage changes color with the seasons.
Moist soil, rich n organic natter, and artial shade re required.	Autumn is the best time to plant. Don't let them dry out before planting. Choose a spot that shades the plants throughout summer.	• Divide the clumps toward the end of summer or in autumn. • For leaves covered in attractive, reddish brown spots, try *E. dens-canis*, with white, purple, or pink flowers, and *E.* 'Pagoda', with yellow flowers.
Moist or even oggy soil, as at he edge of a ond, in part hade or sun.	Ideally, plant in autumn or spring. Feed with high-potassium fertilizer to encourage flowering. Divide established clumps in autumn or early spring.	• For smaller gardens, choose 'Kahome' (2ft/60cm) or *F. palmata* 'Nana' (18in/45cm), both of which have rose-pink flowers. • For a dry site in full sun, try *F. vulgaris*, which has white flowers and thrives in such conditions.
lant in shade r dappled hade in any easonable, ertile soil.	Plant out as soon as any frosts are over, and keep plants well watered. Buy young plants instead of growing from seed, which can be tricky.	• The shadier the conditions, the taller the plants become. In deep shade they become very leggy. • For larger, showy plants consider the New Guinea hybrids, tender perennials that have variegated pink, yellow, and green foliage.
Moist, acidic or eutral soil rich n organic natter, in part r full shade.	Best planted in autumn; add plenty of organic matter to improve moisture retention. Sow seed in a cold frame in autumn.	• Don't be surprised if newly planted trilliums take a while to settle in – this is not unusual. • Some trilliums may be damaged by late frosts, so choose a sheltered spot where possible. • *T. sessile* has scented, reddish brown flowers.
Vell-drained oil, in part hade or sun.	Waldsteinias are easy to grow. Best planted in autumn or spring, they spread rapidly provided the soil is kept moist. Try mixed plantings with bulbs.	• Waldsteinia spreads by producing shoots that then root into the ground, so propagation is easy – just detach rooted sections in late summer. • To ensure plants establish well, grow them in pots until they produce a strong root system.

HINT OF THE ORIENT
The spiky flowers of erythroniums remind me of colorful pagodas as they hang above the often intricately marbled foliage.

LIGHT IN DARKNESS
Bring interest to a shaded corner with the white flower spikes of *Cimifuga simplex* 'Brunette'.

DRESSED IN YELLOW
The golden yellow flowers of *Waldsteinia ternata* make a perfect groundcover for a shaded site. Even when it is not in bloom, its evergreen foliage is attractive.

Flowers for alkaline soil

ALKALINE SOIL TENDS to get bad press, because it's often assumed that few plants really enjoy these conditions. In fact, there are plenty of lovely, cottage garden-style flowers that will actively thrive on alkaline soil, often doing better than they would if your soil were acidic or neutral.

OTHER FLOWERS FOR ALKALINE SOILS

Anemones (*Anemone*) pp.108–109   Peonies (*Paeonia*) pp.54–55
Campanulas (*Campanula*) pp.96–97   Salvias (*Salvia*) pp.74–75
Fritillaries (*Fritillaria*) pp.100–101   Verbascums (*Verbascum*) pp.40–41

PARTNERS IN PINK
Try growing *Dianthus* 'Becky Robinson' with other pink-flowered plants, such as *Lobularia maritima* Easter Bonnet Series *(facing page, top)*.

LA VIE EN ROSE, *right*
Another candidate for a pink grouping, this *Sidalcea* 'Elsie Heugh' combines well with *Physostegia* 'Bouquet Rose', border pinks, valerians, campions, alyssums, or gladioli.

TALL ORDER, *left*
Large gladiolus hybrids such as this 'Georgette' will need stakes to support their flower spikes. To avoid staking, choose dwarf varieties or the smaller, delicate species gladioli.

PLANT	SIZE	APPEARANCE
ANTHEMIS *Anthemis tinctoria* Z 3–7	H 24–32in (60–80cm) S 24–32in (60–80cm)	Ferny, slightly gray-green foliage form attractive backdrop to pretty daisylike flowers in white or yellow, depending the variety. These perennials flower throughout the summer.
VALERIAN *Centranthus ruber* Z 5–8	H 24–30in (60–75cm) S 24–30in (60–75cm)	Clusters of tiny, red or pinkish red flov form compact flowerheads that open throughout summer and into autumn leaves of this perennial are somewhat f and grayish green.
BORDER PINKS *Dianthus* Z 5–9	H 10–16in (25–40cm) S 8–12in (20–30cm)	I can't think of anything prettier than perennials, their flowers like tight, frill rosettes in pink, purple-red, or white, bringing color and scent to the garden throughout early and midsummer.
GLADIOLI *Gladiolus* Z 8–10	H 3–4ft (90–120cm) S 6–8in (15–20cm)	Brilliantly showy flowers in the form c open trumpets are packed into long spil in summer. The flowers come in a wid range of colors including red, pink, ora yellow, purple, and white.
SWEET ALYSSUM *Lobularia maritima* Annual	H 4in (10cm) S 8in (20cm)	Small white, pink, or near-purple flowe are held in rounded groups, forming a almost solid carpet of color for much of summer. Grow it as an annual; it almo always reseeds freely for next year.
OBEDIENT PLANT *Physostegia* Z 4–8	H 4ft (1.2m) S 2ft (60cm)	This rather unusual plant has four-cornered stems topped by spikes of tub flowers in lavender-pink, magenta, or white. A perennial, it flowers from midsummer into autumn.
SIBERIAN SQUILL *Scilla siberica* Z 5–8	H 6–8in (15–20cm) S 2–3in (5–7.5cm)	Delicate blue or white flowers hang lik miniature bells in loose flower spikes i early spring. These bulbs look delightfu planted beneath small shrubs, in containers, and in borders.
CHECKER MALLOWS *Sidalcea* Z 5–8	H 2–3ft (60–90cm) S 20in (50cm)	Looking like a cross between shrubby mallows (*Lavatera*) and hollyhocks, thes perennials produce spires of open, fun shaped flowers in pink or white from r to late summer.
CAMPION *Silene schafta* Z 5–7	H 6in (15cm) S 12in (30cm)	This semievergreen perennial produce constant supply of pretty, pale pink flo to top spreading tufts of midgreen foli from the middle of summer until early midautumn.
GOLDENROD *Solidago* Z 5–9	H 18–48in (45–120cm) S 10–24in (25–60cm)	As their common name suggests, the prominent feature of these cheerful perennials is their golden yellow flowe spikes that are produced from summe into autumn.

ITE	CULTIVATION	HINTS AND TIPS
Choose a sunny spot with well-drained soil.	Best planted in spring or autumn. Plants generally do not require any support. Divide established clumps in spring to reinvigorate them.	• Cut back faded flower stems to keep plants looking good and to encourage further flowering. • Best planted in groups of odd numbers in a herbaceous border. • For white flowers, look for *A. tinctoria* 'Alba'.
Well-drained alkaline soil in plenty of sun.	Ideally, plant in spring or autumn on very well-drained soil. Divide established clumps in spring every third or fourth year.	• Valerian thrives on poor soil, so avoid feeding it or planting it in ground rich in nutrients. If overfed, the plants tend to become leggy and are best replaced. • A great plant for attracting butterflies.
Any reasonably well-drained, fertile soil in full sun or part shade.	Planting in early or midautumn is best. Unlike carnations, pinks should not need support. Take cuttings from nonflowering side-shoots in early to midsummer.	• Feed moderately to keep plants in good condition and flowering well. Replace once they have become straggly, after a few years. • Pinch out the shoot tips of young plants in spring to stimulate bushy growth.
A sunny site with well-drained soil is required.	Their corms are best planted in spring, 6in (15cm) deep and 4–8in (10–20cm) apart. Manure before planting, and add sand if the soil is not very free-draining.	• Where not hardy, lift the corms in autumn and dry off in a frost-free place. Clear off debris and store until the following spring. • Cormlets that are removed and grown on will take up to three years to reach flowering size.
Well-drained soil and plenty of sun.	Sow seeds in early spring in pots or trays in a cold greenhouse or cold frame. Plant out toward the end of spring. Alternatively, sow direct.	• Alyssums self-seed readily; named varieties will not come true but still produce a good show. • For different, striking colors, try 'Oriental Night', 'Apricot Shades', 'Wonderland Red', 'Rosie O'Day', and 'Royal Carpet'.
Plant in a moist soil rich in organic matter in sun or dappled shade.	Best planted in autumn or spring. Add plenty of compost or leafmold if your soil is light. Keep watered in dry spells and mulch around the base, too.	• This lovely, rapidly growing plant may spread too quickly, so be prepared to divide it every year or two, in spring or autumn. • For bright pink flowers choose 'Vivid'; 'Summer Snow' and 'Crown of Snow' have white flowers.
Moisture-retaining yet free-draining soil in dappled shade is ideal.	Plant the bulbs toward the end of summer or in early autumn, at a depth and spacing of 2–3in (5–7.5cm). Add leafmold to encourage moisture retention.	• Squills look good if allowed to naturalize; plant at uneven spacings in a driftlike shape. • To increase your stock or replace plants, divide congested clumps every four years or so. • For bright white flowers choose 'Alba'.
Choose a sunny or part shaded site in any fairly fertile and moist soil.	Checker mallows are very easy to grow. Ideally, plant in autumn or spring. In dry weather water well and apply a mulch. Divide in spring or autumn.	• For really silky-looking midpink flowers choose 'Rose Queen'. *S. candida* has white flowers. • Species can be raised from seed sown in a cold frame or cold greenhouse in early spring. • Checker mallows make good cut flowers.
Plant in well-drained, fertile soil, in full sun.	Best planted in spring or autumn, campions require little attention. Sow seeds early in spring, or divide established plants in autumn.	• I especially like the variety 'Shell Pink', in a particularly delicate shade. • The flowers attract both butterflies and bees and are especially well suited to plantings with an informal or even wild feel to them.
Choose a sunny or part shaded spot with well-drained yet moist soil.	Ideally, plant in spring or autumn. They are easy to look after and should not need staking. Divide established clumps every three or four years.	• During dry weather ensure that the soil does not dry out completely. • For a small, compact plant choose 'Golden Thumb' (also known as 'Queenie'), which flowers in late summer.

QUICK AND EASY
Easily raised from seed, alyssums – here *Lobularia maritima* Easter Bonnet Series – grow rapidly to create a low-growing carpet of color. They are also an excellent way to fill gaps between paving or along path edging.

HIGH JINKS
Physostegias are excellent plants for the middle or back of a border. You can have them in white or go for a variety such as this 'Bouquet Rose', which has pretty lilac-pink spikes.

Flowers for containers

BY GROWING FLOWERS IN containers you can plant what you like, regardless of the soil in your garden. Barrels and pots also allow you to get the best from plants in small spaces, since those past their best can be removed so that flowers in season can take center stage.

OTHER FLOWERS FOR CONTAINERS

HIGH FLIERS
With their tendency to grow up then sprawl over, *Brachyscome iberidifolia* varieties – here 'White Splendour' – are ideal for growing in containers.

Geraniums bring height to the planting

ROSE-TINTED VIEW, *below*
I find most petunias grown on their own too bright for my taste, but combined with more subtle pink flowers these look perfect.

Deadhead petunias often

Terracotta pot coordinates with flower colors

PLANT	SIZE		APPEARANCE
TUBEROUS BEGONIAS *Begonia* min 50°F (10°C)	H 12–24in (30–60cm)	S 12in (30cm)	The flowers of begonias range from sm and delicate to big beauties resembling camellias and may be white, pink, red, yellow, orange, or cream. They are bor throughout summer and into early autu
BIDENS *Bidens ferulifolia* Z 8–10	H 18–24in (45–60cm)	S 18in (45cm)	The combination of starry, daisylike, br yellow flowers and ferny foliage makes bidens a superb container plant for the summer. Although perennials, they are best grown as annuals.
SWAN RIVER DAISY *Brachyscome iberidifolia* Annual	H 6–12in (15–30cm)	S 6–12in (15–30cm)	One word sums up these delightful dais giddy! The flowers of these bushy annu come in white, blue, or purple, all with bright yellow center, and appear throughout the summer.
FUCHSIAS *Fuchsia* mostly Z 8–10	Extremely variable, so check label for details.		Pendulous flowers resembling bells or elaborate ballerina skirts in white, red, purple, pink, or lilac cover the plants throughout summer and into autumn. T perennials may be grown as annuals.
HEBES *Hebe* Z 8–11	H 12–36in (30–90cm)	S 12–30in (30–75cm)	Provided you choose small species or varieties, these pretty evergreen plants great in containers. Flower spikes in wh or shades of pink, red, purple, or blue develop from spring into autumn.
LOBELIA *Lobelia erinus* Annual	H 6in (15cm)	S 6in (15cm)	Countless tiny jewel-like flowers, in pa pastels, white, or bright shades of blue, pink, or lilac, cover the stems of this annual in a constant stream of color fro the end of spring until the first frosts.
GERANIUMS *Pelargonium* Usually annual	H 12–24in (30–60cm)	S 8–18in (20–45cm)	The many types of geranium are all goo containers. Many flower profusely, usu right through summer, in white, pink, or purple; some have beautifully colore shaped, or scented leaves, too.
PETUNIAS *Petunia* Annual	H 8–12in (20–30cm)	S 12–20in (30–50cm)	These uncomplicated, showy plants off single or double, wide-open trumpet-shaped flowers in white, yellow, pink, r violet, cream – even green – from early summer until the first frosts.
PORTULACA *Portulaca grandiflora* Annual	H 6–8in (15–20cm)	S 8in (20cm)	As if made from the brightest colored s these open, roselike flowers dazzle in shocking pink, red, yellow, orange, or white. This annual blooms from summ until midautumn.
VERBENA *Verbena* Z 4–11; others annual	H 8–10in (20–25cm)	S 12in (30cm)	Rounded flowerheads in white or shad of pink, purple, cream, or red are produced from midsummer until the f frosts. Annuals and perennials, includ upright and trailing forms.

TE	CULTIVATION	HINTS AND TIPS
easonably ell-drained, rtile, moist il mix in appled shade.	Buy as growing plants, or start tubers into growth in pots of fresh soil mix in early spring. Plant out after any late frosts. Keep soil mix moist but not wet.	• Feed with high-potassium fertilizer. • Begonias are not sun-lovers, so use them in pots where they will look their best – in dappled shade. • Once plants have died back in autumn, overwinter tubers in dry soil mix in a frost-free shed.
appy in sun part shade, any asonable soil soil mix.	Buy as plants, or raise your own by sowing seed in a propagating case in early spring. Harden off plants and plant out after any danger of late frosts.	• Pinch out the shoot tips of small, home-raised plants when they are 2–3in (5–8cm) tall to increase branching and bushiness. • Try 'Golden Goddess', which seems to thrive in all the extremes of summer weather.
ell-drained il mix in a ery sunny, referably eltered spot.	Buy as plants in spring, or sow seed in early spring. Grow plants on and harden off before planting out in late spring. Deadhead regularly to prolong flowering.	• Species and taller varieties may flop over – use twiggy prunings as unobtrusive supports. • Create a drift of hazy, daisy color using a single variety. I look for 'Splendour White' or 'Splendour Purple'.
ell-drained il mix in sun part shade.	Ideally, plant out after any danger of late frosts. Keep well watered and fed, and deadhead regularly. Softwood cuttings taken in late spring root readily.	• Pinching out the tips of the shoots early in the season increases bushiness. • Always check whether plants are hardy or not. Mulch hardy plants in winter; lift tender ones and overwinter in a cool but frost-free greenhouse.
eed plenty sun and ell-drained il mix.	Hebes are best planted in autumn or spring. They dislike both too much and too little water; good drainage and regular watering are essential.	• Take semiripe heeled cuttings toward the end of summer. • Add spring- or autumn-flowering plants at the base of the hebe for a long season of color. • Cut straggly stems back hard each spring.
ell-drained il mix, kept oist, in full n or part ade.	Buy as plants, or sow seed very early in spring in a propagating case. Prick out, grow on, and harden off before planting out once danger of frosts is over.	• Keep lobelia well watered and fed. • Seedlings are prone to damping-off disease, so water seed trays and young plants with a copper-based fungicide at regular intervals. • Discard plants once they start to look ratty.
equire well-rained soil ix in a sunny osition.	Buy as plants, or raise from seed sown in late winter or from softwood cuttings taken in spring or summer. Harden off before planting out after any late frosts.	• Geraniums need plenty of feeding. • Deadhead regularly to encourage more blooms and reduce the risk of gray mold infection. • Choose ivy-leaved forms for hanging baskets, windowboxes, or the edges of large pots.
hrive in ell-drained il mix in enty of sun.	Buy as plants or sow seed in early spring in a propagating case on the surface of the soil mix. Prick out, harden off, and plant out after any late frosts.	• Feed with a high-potassium fertilizer. • The small, pretty flowers of the Carillon Series give a more delicate effect. • Trailing forms can be taller (up to 16in/40cm) and spread out up to 3ft (90cm).
ee-draining il mix in enty of sun.	Readily available as plants, or sow seed in a propagating case in early spring, prick out, and harden off before planting out after any late frosts.	• Beware of overfeeding. Given too rich a lifestyle, these annuals flower less profusely. • Also great as a summer groundcover. • If you fancy a double-flowered form, look for the F2 hybrid 'Calypso'.
eed plenty of n, and will rive in most ils or soil ixes.	Buy as plants, or sow seed in a propagating case in early spring. Take softwood cuttings in early summer if seed is unavailable, and overwinter in a greenhouse.	• After sowing, keep seed in the dark in a propagating case to increase success of germination. • To prevent powdery mildew, spray with a suitable fungicide. • 'Silver Anne' (pale pink) is a good trailing form.

Ivy-leaved geranium

Purple-pink verbena *Trailing lobelia*

FULL OF PROMISE
Hanging baskets should be crammed with lots of plants and kept well fed and watered.

ENDURING APPEAL
An evergreen hebe – here *Hebe* 'Bowles Variety' – provides year-round interest.

RUNNING WILD, *below*
Trailing stems can be used to create a pretty effect in containers.

Pale lilac lobelia *Trailing helichrysum*

Pot feet ensure good drainage

Flowers for cutting

IF YOU HAVE THE SPACE, it's lovely to be able to grow flowers specifically for cutting to display indoors. Although most garden flowers can be picked, some are particularly well suited to life in both the border and the vase. By growing your own, you can guarantee your favorites for the home.

OTHER FLOWERS FOR CUTTING

Hollyhocks (*Alcea rosea*) pp.44–45
Alliums (*Allium*) pp.50–51
Sunflowers (*Helianthus*) pp.82–83

Peonies (*Paeonia*) pp.54–55
Sweet peas (*Lathyrus odoratus*) pp.56–57
Lilies (*Lilium*) pp.62–63

KINGPINS *above*
With the bold, bright flowers of *Arctotis fastuosa* 'Monarch of the Veldt' – each bloom up to 2in (5cm) across – you can bring warmth to any room.

BATS IN THE BELFRY, *left*
It is easy to see why *Moluccella laevis* is sometimes known as shell flower. With their somewhat eerie appearance, the flowers also remind me of green bats' ears.

PLANT	SIZE	APPEARANCE
YARROW *Achillea* Z 4–9	H 3ft (90cm) S 2ft (60cm)	Large, round, flattened flowerheads (e up to 6in /15cm across), made up of numerous tiny, bright yellow flowers a produced from midsummer to early autumn by this perennial.
PERUVIAN LILIES *Alstroemeria* Z 7–10	H 12–40in (30–100cm) S 12–36in (30–90cm)	These exotic, orchidlike flowers are no really difficult to grow. They bloom from midsummer into late autumn in white, cream, shades of red, orange, yellow, or lavender.
AFRICAN DAISIES *Arctotis × hybrida* Annual	H 12–18in (30–45cm) S 12in (30cm)	These startlingly beautiful daisylike flov come in white, red, orange, cream, pink reddish brown, and bloom for much o summer. Although perennials, they ar grown as annuals in most areas.
CROWN IMPERIALS *Fritillaria imperialis* Z 5–9	H 5ft (1.5m) S 12in (30cm)	Unusual and striking cut flowers, crow imperials have tall flower spikes each bearing a ring of hanging, tulip-shaped flowers in red, orange, or yellow, topp with a tuft of leafy bracts, in spring.
BABY'S BREATH *Gypsophila paniculata* Z 4–9	H 2–4ft (60–120cm) S 10–40in (25–100cm)	No flower arranger would want to be without baby's breath, with its large, ai delicate sprays of tiny flowers in white pale pink. This perennial flowers from midsummer to midautumn.
BEARDED IRISES *Iris* Z 6–9	H 2–3ft (60–90cm) S 10–12in (25–30cm)	These irises have varieties in almost an color you could wish for. They all have branched flower stems, bearing about s flowers, usually with a pleasant perfun in midspring.
WINTER JASMINE *Jasminum nudiflorum* Z 6–9	H 13–15ft (4–4.5m) S 6–7ft (1.8–2.1m)	A welcome sight in the depths of winte pale yellow flowers break out over dar green stems at intervals from the end c autumn until early spring. This plant is trained as a scrambler against a wall.
BELLS OF IRELAND *Moluccella laevis* Annual	H 2–3ft (60–90cm) S 12in (30cm)	Although its tall stems appear to bear bright green trumpet flowers, these are fact green collars that encase the tiny, w fragrant flowers. This annual flowers fr midsummer to early autumn.
CHINESE LANTERNS *Physalis alkekengi* Z 5–8	H 2–3ft (60–90cm) S 2–3ft (60–90cm)	Like honesty, physalis is grown as muc its seedcases as for its flowers – bright orange-red, lantern-shaped papery bla that develop around an inner orange b A fast-growing, invasive perennial.
SCABIOSA *Scabiosa caucasica* Z 4–9	H 18–24in (45–60cm) S 18–24in (45–60cm)	Sometimes known as pincushion flower annual blooms in lavender, off-white, best of all, a really true, pale Wedgwood throughout most of the summer. Self-s seedlings may produce beautiful varian

TE	CULTIVATION	HINTS AND TIPS
'ell-drained oil with plenty f sun.	Plant purchased plants in early spring, or sow seed in a propagating case in late winter or very early spring. Divide established plants in early spring.	• In exposed conditions, some support for the stems may be necessary. • My absolute favorite for cutting is *A. filipendulina* 'Cloth of Gold'. • Yarrows make good dried flowers.
'ell-drained oil, in a heltered, unny spot.	Before planting, dig in compost. Plant once any late frosts are over; the top of each tuberous root should be about 1in (2.5cm) below the surface.	• Divide established clumps in spring. • In autumn, mulch the crowns with a deep layer of bark chips to provide winter protection. • For best results as a cut flower, pick as soon as the first flowers on the stem open.
ree-draining oil and plenty f sun.	Buy as plants, or sow seed in a cold frame in spring. Plant out after any late frosts, watering in well. Once established give an occasional high-potassium feed.	• In dull weather and as evening approaches these flowers often close, but they'll open as soon as the sun is out again. • Seeds are available in single or mixed colors, and they all make great cut flowers.
airly heavy oil, in sun or art shade.	Plant in autumn, incorporating lots of coarse compost to improve fertility and soil texture. Keep them well fed and well watered.	• Crown imperials are difficult to propagate at home, so it is best to buy new bulbs. • They dislike being disturbed and may fail to flower if not allowed to become well established. • The flowers smell skunky (unpleasant to some).
leeds a well-rained, ideally lkaline or eutral soil and lenty of sun.	Best planted in early spring. Tall varieties will need support; twiggy sticks are unobtrusive. Take softwood cuttings in early summer.	• Removing the flowering stems for use as cut flowers will actually stimulate the plant to produce more. • For a compact plant, try 'Festival White'. 'Bristol Fairy' has double white flowers.
'ell-drained oil, slightly cidic, with lenty of sun.	Plant the rhizomes between midsummer and early autumn, setting them so that the top of the rhizome is just barely below the surface of the soil.	• Clumps can be divided every two to four years; discard the old, central rhizomes and replant newer sections. • Water regularly for the first three or four weeks after planting.
'ell-drained oil close to a vall or other ertical surface f any exposure.	Best planted in autumn or spring. Winter jasmine makes an excellent covering for a wall, but it will need a support up which to scramble.	• Semiripe cuttings taken in mid- to late summer usually root very easily. • To force early flowering, bring stems into a cool room just as the flower buds have started to fatten and then at intervals throughout the winter.
Choose a sunny pot with well-rained, fertile oil.	Sow seed in a propagating case in early spring, harden off, and plant out after any late frosts. In mild areas, try direct sowing in the flowering site in midspring.	• Bells of Ireland not only makes a great cut flower, it also adds interest to any border and can be used in dried arrangements, too. • For drying, cut stems before they start to fade and hang upside down in a well-ventilated spot.
Thrives on any easonable arden soil, in ull sun or part hade.	Best planted in autumn or spring. Divide established plants in winter or early spring. If the stems flop, don't bother staking; it suits them to look informal.	• Given the right conditions, Chinese lanterns can be invasive, so control if necessary by using a sharp spade to cut around the roots each autumn. • They can also be dried, held upright to ensure that the lanterns dry pointing downward.
'ell-drained oil, in plenty f sun.	Sow seed during spring direct into their flowering positions and thin out to 18–24in (45–60cm) apart. Deadhead regularly if necessary.	• Bees and butterflies are attracted to these flowers. • For really intense blue flowers try 'Fama'; it has long flower stems, which makes it particularly good for tall arrangements.

RURAL CHARMS
Introduce a relaxed, country air into the home with a bunch of delightfully informal scabiosa in a simple jug.

NET GAIN, *right*
Even when dried physalis seedcases start to disintegrate, they leave a fascinating netlike "lantern."

CROWNED HEADS
I love crown imperials for bold arrangements, but not in small rooms — the scent is a bit overpowering! Try them in the hall or on the landing.

Dried flowers and seedheads

FLOWERS THAT DRY WELL give pleasure all year round, and attractive seedheads look great in arrangements, too. Grow plenty of these so you can leave some on the plant over winter; they'll look dramatic covered in a heavy frost, and birds often appreciate the seeds, too.

OTHER FLOWERS FOR DRIED ARRANGEMENTS

Hollyhocks (*Alcea rosea*) pp.44–45
Alliums (*Allium*) pp.50–51
Dictamnus albus pp.130–131

Lavenders (*Lavandula*) pp.70–71
Nigellas (*Nigella*) pp.72–73
Physalis alkekengi pp.150–151

LUNAR LEGACY, *left and below*
This *Lunaria annua* 'Variegata' provides interest for many months, with its smartly variegated foliage and pretty pink flowers, followed by silvery seedheads in autumn.

Seeds are produced on silvery dollars

HIGH AND DRY, *right*
In summer *Echinops ritro* 'Veitch's Blue' bears globes of tiny purple-lilac flowers, fragments of which remain on faded flowerheads left on the plant.

PLANT	SIZE	APPEARANCE
BEAR'S BREECHES *Acanthus mollis* Z 7–10	H 4ft (1.2m) S 3ft (90cm)	This perennial has large, architectural, divided leaves that die back in autumn reappear again in spring. The stately fl spikes in pink and white that appear i early summer are excellent for drying
WINGED EVERLASTING *Ammobium alatum* Annual	H 18–24in (45–60cm) S 18in (45cm)	This annual produces masses of small, silvery white everlasting-type flowers, e of which has a large, bright yellow cent The flowers are produced on winged st from early summer to midautumn.
PEARLY EVERLASTING *Anaphalis margaritacea* Z 4-8	H 24–30in (60–75cm) S 24–30in (60–75cm)	From midsummer into autumn this fa growing perennial is studded with clu of small, papery, white flowers that dr well. The foliage is downy-felted and s appears silvery gray.
GLOBE THISTLES *Echinops* Z 4–9	H 4–6ft (1.2–1.8m) S 12–36in (30–90m)	Spiky, spherical flowerheads in metalli blue to purple are produced on these growing perennials from midsummer early autumn. They look very eye-catc in dried displays.
STINKING IRIS *Iris foetidissima* Z 7–9	H 20in (50cm) S 12in (30cm)	Although its grayish pink early-summ flowers are attractive, the stinking iris reserves a bolder display for autumn, stunning seedpods that split open to r bright orange-red or yellow seeds.
STRAWFLOWERS *Helichrysum bracteatum* Annual	H 16–60in (40–150cm) S 12–16in (30–40cm)	Best grown as annuals, strawflowers pr an array of yellow, gold, pink-orange, reddish brown flowers from midsumm midautumn. The flower petals are so papery that they dry particularly well.
STATICE *Limonium sinuatum* Annual	H 12–24in (30–60cm) S 12in (30cm)	Statice grows wild on Mediterranean c withstanding hot, salty winds – perfec drying conditions. From midsummer early autumn, the elongated flower cl appear in purple, yellow, white, red, or
HONESTY, SILVER DOLLARS *Lunaria annua* Z 5–9	H 3ft (90cm) S 2ft (60cm)	While the white or purple flowers produced by honesty in early summer pretty, it's the green and, later, silvery cream disklike seed cases of this bienni that really catch the eye.
FEVERFEW *Matricaria* Z 4–9	H 6–24in (15–60cm) S 6–18in (15–45cm)	These short-lived perennials flower throughout the summer, producing da like single or fluffy double flowers in w or yellow. The bushy foliage is a lovely green, with a smell you either love or
JERUSALEM SAGE *Phlomis fruticosa* Z 8–9	H 3ft (90cm) S 3ft (90cm)	With its clusters of hooded flowers, thi reminds me of an oversized deadnettle with silvery leaves. Bright yellow flowe are formed through the summer on th shrubby evergreen.

ITE	CULTIVATION	HINTS AND TIPS
Well-drained soil, ideally in full sun, or if not in light shade.	Plant in spring, incorporating sand if the soil has a tendency to become wet in winter. The easiest method of propagation is by division in spring.	• In cold areas, mulch the crown with bark chips to provide winter protection. • Very prone to powdery mildew disease; if attacks occur early in the season, consider spraying with a suitable fungicide.
Requires well-drained soil and plenty of sun.	Sow seed in a propagating case from late winter to early spring. Harden off, then plant out after any danger of frost. They need little watering once established.	• Cut just as most of the flowers on the stem are starting to open. • Like other everlasting-type flowers, it is best to tie them loosely into bunches and dry by hanging upside down in a well-ventilated spot.
Well-drained yet moisture-retentive soil, in plenty of sun.	Plant out in autumn or early spring (spring is better if there is any tendency for the soil to be wet over winter). Water well during dry weather.	• Established plants can be divided in spring or autumn. • For smaller spaces, choose the more compact variety 'Neuschnee', which grows to only 18in (45cm) tall, with a similar spread.
Choose a sunny spot with well-drained soil.	Plant in autumn or spring; add sand if the soil is not well drained. Divide established clumps in spring or autumn, or take root cuttings at the end of autumn.	• Globe thistles attract bees, butterflies, and birds. • They perform well in very dry conditions and on poor or alkaline soils. • Best picked for drying just before the tiny purple flowers appear.
Needs a reasonably moist soil, in part shade.	Plant toward the end of summer or in early autumn. Divide established clumps in autumn, or gather and sow seeds direct into the flowering site.	• Cut the stems bearing the seedheads just as the pods start to split. Dry them standing up, or else the seeds will all fall out. • The foliage has an unpleasant smell when cut or crushed.
Free-draining soil and plenty of sun.	Plant out in spring. Seed can be sown direct into the flowering position in early to midspring, or sown in a propagating case in early spring.	• Tall varieties may need some support if grown in an exposed position. • Cut for drying just before the flowers are fully open and hang in bunches in a well-ventilated spot.
Well-drained, alkaline or neutral soil, in full sun.	Plant out in spring after any late frosts. Single- or mixed-color plants may be raised from seed sown in a propagating case in early spring.	• Dry in bunches hung in a well-ventilated spot. • For smaller gardens, choose 'Dwarf Biedermeier Strain', which grows to only 10–12in (25–30cm). • 'Pastel Shades' offers more subtle colors. • May also be used as fresh cut flowers.
Likes a well-drained soil, in dappled shade.	Best planted in autumn or spring; easy to grow. Sow seeds direct where they are to flower in spring or early summer for flowers the following year.	• No need to stake. • Cut the flower stems in summer before seeds have ripened fully, to prevent them from being spoiled by rain or winds. • 'Alba Variegata' has attractive variegated foliage.
Well-drained soil, in full sun or part shade.	Sow seed in spring in a propagating case. Harden off, then plant out after any danger of frost. Plants also self-seed readily once established.	• Two of my favorites are 'Butterball', which has dense yellow flowers, and 'Bridal Robe', which has double, bright white flowers. • Cut just as the flowers start to open fully and dry in bunches in a well-ventilated spot.
Choose a site in full sun with well-drained soil.	Plant in spring; add plenty of sand in all but the most well-drained soils. No need to prune regularly. Take semiripe cuttings in late summer or autumn.	• Winter moisture quickly kills Jerusalem sage, so if necessary take cuttings and overwinter them in well-drained soil mix in a cold frame. • Leave some flower stems on plants in the border to be decorated by frost.

Spikelets bear tiny, papery flowers

BRIGHT SPARKS
The bright flower colors of *Limonium sinuatum* Fortress Series (*above*) and 'Forever Gold' (*above right*) are retained well upon drying.

Cases split to reveal the seeds

Seedhead of *Iris foetidissima*

GREAT BALLS OF FIRE, *above*
The flowers of *Iris foetidissima* — here *I. foetidissima* var. *citrina* — are interesting, but the plant's greatest attraction is the bright scarlet or yellow seeds that burst from the large seed pods in autumn.

FOREVER YOUNG, *right*
All strawflowers provide long-lasting color once dried and will start to fade noticeably only after a couple of years. These are from the King Size series.

Winter and early spring flowers

ALTHOUGH I QUITE enjoy winter, I find myself waiting with bated breath for the first sight of snowdrops that tell me spring is on its way. Even in the depths of winter, there's no need for your garden to close down completely – even one or two plants in flower make all the difference.

OTHER FLOWERS FOR WINTER AND EARLY SPRING

Anemones (*Anemone blanda*) pp.108 – 109
Hellebores (*Helleborus*) pp.114 – 115
Stinking iris (*Iris foetidissima*) pp.152 – 153
Daffodils (*Narcissus*) pp.104 – 105
Jasminum nudiflorum pp.150 – 151
Violas (*Violas*) pp.116 – 117

FLOWER POWER
The flowers of *Cyclamen coum* and *Galanthus nivalis* may be tiny, but they have a huge impact in the winter garden, when little else is in bloom.

STARSTRUCK, *below*
The bright flower colors of crocuses – here, 'Advance' – never cease to amaze me; they seem more in keeping with summer than with winter and early spring. On sunny days, the flowers open like tiny stars.

PLANT	SIZE	APPEARANCE
ENGLISH DAISIES *Bellis perennis* Z 4–8	H 6–8in (15–20cm) S 8in (20cm)	These jaunty English daisies pop up in early spring, their pink, red, or white flowers looking like so many miniatur drumsticks. You can enjoy these bienn until early summer.
WALLFLOWERS *Cheiranthus cheiri* Z 3–7	H 8–18in (20–45cm) S 6–8in (15–20cm)	For color and fragrance wallflowers ha few rivals; biennials with dense spikes delicately scented flowers in warm sha of red, yellow, orange, purple, or bron from early spring until early summer.
CROCUSES *Crocus* Z 3–8	H 2¾–4in (7–10cm) S 2–3in (5–7.5cm)	The brightly colored, cup-shaped flow these small, hardy corms are a welcom sight in late winter and spring. Crocus can be single colors such as white, crea or purple, or a combination of colors.
CYCLAMEN *Cyclamen coum* Z 5–9	H 2–3in (5–7.5cm) S 6in (15cm)	Charm epitomized! From midwinter t early spring these plants produce smal winged flowers in shades of pink, from pale to screaming magenta. The leaves be plain green or silver-patterned.
WINTER ACONITE *Eranthis hyemalis* Z 4–9	H 6in (15cm) S 6in (15cm)	Golden yellow buttercup-like flowers, with a bright green "ruff," develop fro this tuber. The flowers look breathtaki beautiful beneath shrubs or trees from winter into early spring.
HEATHERS *Erica carnea* Z 5–7	H 6–12in (15–30cm) S 10–24in (25–60cm)	These make a showy, easy-care groundc Compact but numerous flower spikes i white or shades of pink or purple are produced over a mound of evergreen fo throughout winter and into early sprir
SNOWDROPS *Galanthus nivalis* Z 3–9	H 4–8in (10–20cm) S 2–4in (5–10cm)	Just seeing these little white bells appe from winter into early spring reminds that winter cold has its compensations. flowers of this bulb have pretty green markings on their inner petals.
EARLY IRISES *Iris reticulata* Z 5–8	H 6–8in (15–20cm) S 3–4in (7.5–10cm)	Despite their diminutive stature, these irises are difficult to miss! Blue, purple, near-white flowers are marked with bri yellow and bring a dazzling display to t garden in late winter and into early spr
SPRING SNOWFLAKE *Leucojum vernum* Z 4–8	H 8–10in (20–25cm) S 6–8in (15–20cm)	An elegant relative of the snowdrop, sp snowflake has nodding, bell-shaped wh flowers with a distinct green spot on th point of each petal. This bulb flowers f late winter to early spring.
PASQUEFLOWERS *Pulsatilla vulgaris* Z 5–7	H 8in (20cm) S 6in (15cm)	One of the most distinctive features of pasqueflowers is the silky down that co their stems and flowers. Delicate bell-sh flowers appear from early spring in wh pinkish red, or purple, with golden stan

SITE	CULTIVATION	HINTS AND TIPS
Fairly well-drained soil, in either sun or part shade.	Bedding plants may be available, or sow seeds in a propagating case between late spring and midsummer for flowering the following year.	• Remove faded flowers regularly to encourage new ones to form. • Pomponette Mixed is a pretty mixture to raise from seed. It is particularly compact and has strong colors.
Any reasonable soil, including alkaline, in sun or part shade.	Available as plants, or sow seeds outdoors between midspring and early summer. Pinch out growing tips when plants are 3–4in (7.5–10cm) tall.	• Pinch out the shoot tips of young plants to encourage good, bushy growth. • The delicate perfume of wallflowers will attract bees into the garden. • Try growing them with tulips in strong colors.
Choose a sunny spot with well-drained soil.	Plant the corms as soon as they are available, usually in autumn. Planting depth varies with corm size, but generally 2in (5cm) is usually enough.	• Crocuses look best planted in miniature drifts, randomly spaced to look natural. • Try naturalizing crocuses on a grassy bank. Instead of making individual holes, lift sections of sod, plant corms into the soil beneath, and replace.
Moist yet well-drained soil, in dappled shade or sun.	Buy either as pot-grown plants or tubers. Plant preferably in late summer or early autumn, placing tubers 1–2in (2.5–5cm) below the soil surface.	• Apply leafmold or compost every autumn to keep soil in good condition. • Cyclamens are often collected from the wild, damaging native habitats in the process. Check that yours are from a cultivated source.
Fairly well-drained soil, in sun, part shade or shade.	Soak the wizened-looking tubers in tepid water for a few hours before planting. The foliage dies down in summer, so always interplant with summer flowers.	• If you have problems establishing winter aconites from tubers, specialized nurseries sometimes supply them "in the green" (plants lifted shortly after flowering while still in leaf). Although more expensive, these are generally easier to get started.
Will tolerate a wide range of soils, in part shade or, ideally, full sun.	Best planted in spring or autumn. Incorporate leafmold or compost on planting to ensure that the soil doesn't get too dry. Water in dry weather.	• After flowering, trim lightly to keep plants really dense and compact. • As a groundcover, they look best planted in groups of several plants of the same color, odd numbers if possible.
Choose any spot in shade with reasonable soil, not too damp nor too dry.	Plant the bulbs in early autumn – about 4in (10cm) deep – in miniature drifts under trees and shrubs. When clumps become congested, lift and divide.	• If establishing snowdrops from bulbs proves tricky, obtain them "in the green" (just after flowering and still in leaf) from a specialized nursery. Check that snowdrops sold as bulbs have not been collected from the wild.
Well-drained soil, in plenty of sun.	Plant the bulbs as soon as they become available in garden centers and nurseries (usually early autumn) at a depth of 3–5in (7.5–12 cm).	• To encourage a good show the following year, feed with a high-potassium fertilizer every two or three weeks as soon as the flowers start to fade. • Choose among the many named varieties for variations in color.
Well-drained yet moisture-retentive soil, in dappled shade.	Plant the bulbs as soon as they are available, usually in autumn, at a depth of 2–4in (5–10cm). They thrive on being left where they are for years.	• To keep them flowering well, make sure that the soil is neither boggy nor allowed to become too dry. • Congested clumps can be divided for more plants. Lift and divide as the leaves turn yellow.
Must have a sunny spot with free-draining soil, ideally alkaline.	Best planted in spring or autumn. Incorporate sand into the soil to improve drainage. Species can be raised from seed, but named varieties will not come true.	• Deadheading helps prolong the flowering period; toward the end, leave some of the fluffy seedheads on the plant to enjoy. • I love 'Rubra' (rich red), 'Alba' (white), and 'Barton's Pink' (delicate shell pink).

COLD COMFORT
The courageous little winter aconite will flower in the chilliest conditions: its silky golden petals stand proud even in snow.

TAMED SPIRITS
Although you may shun its wild relatives, *Bellis perennis* – here Tasso Series – is a great plant for containers or borders from early spring onward.

Flower markings just like little sparkling eyes

A LA MODE
There are many varieties of *Iris reticulata* available, in a range of striking shades – this is 'J. S. Dijt', in regal purple. Add them to spring containers for their richness of color and elegant form. Some have a subtle yet distinct perfume.

Late summer and autumn flowers

ALL TOO OFTEN, FLOWER borders come to a crashing halt by late summer – everything starts to look tired and sorry for itself. By adding some late-season performers to your garden, you can keep color and brightness going well into autumn and so prolong the life of your display.

OTHER LATE-SEASON FLOWERS

Perennial asters (*Aster*) pp.78–79	Rock roses (*Helianthemum*) pp.138–139
Coreopsis (*Coreopsis*) pp.138–139	Penstemons (*Penstemon*) pp.34–35
Gazanias (*Gazania*) pp.140–141	Rudbeckias (*Rudbeckia*) pp.88–89

AUTUMN COLOR
The long, trumpet-shaped, fiery flowers of *Crocosmia*, packed along elegant stems, bring true autumn warmth to beds and borders. Fans of sword-shaped leaves in bright green make a vivid contrast.

Compact buds open into star-shaped flowers

PASTEL POWER
Large, flattened heads of small flowers, usually in shades of pink, sit above the cool, pale, succulent leaves of *Sedum spectabile*. On warm days they are covered with butterflies and bees.

PLANT	SIZE	APPEARANCE
ANEMONES *Anemone × hybrida, A. hupehensis* Z 4–8	H 30–60in (75–150cm) S 18–24in (45–60cm)	For late summer and autumn flowering performance, these anemones are difficult to beat. Their shell-like petals, usually in white, pink, or lilac-pink, surround a circle of golden stamens.
GARDEN MUMS *Chrysanthemum* Hardiness varies	H 18–36in (45–90cm) S 12–18in (30–45cm)	Think rich, think showy – chrysanthemums are both, and more! From late summer into early autumn these often marginally hardy perennials are a blaze of golds, bronzes, yellows, oranges, pinks, and reds.
FALL CROCUSES *Colchicum* Z 4–9	H 6–10in (15–25cm) S 4–6in (10–15cm)	Not the crocuses of spring but relatives of the lily, fall crocuses produce leaves rather than flowers in spring and the foliage dies down by summer. They are perfect for naturalizing in grass or for underplanting.
MONTBRETIAS *Crocosmia* Z 6–9	H 18–36in (45–90cm) S 4–6in (10–15cm)	The fiery reds, oranges, and yellows of autumn foliage are captured in the funnel-shaped flowers of montbretias, carried on arching spikes. These corms bloom in late summer and early autumn.
CONEFLOWERS *Echinacea purpurea* Z 3–9	H 3–5ft (90–150cm) S 20in (50cm)	These daisylike flowers in white, pink, or purple make an excellent foil for the more exuberant late-flowering plants. Perennials, they are a late-season treat for bees and butterflies.
HELENIUMS *Helenium* Z 4–8	H 3–4ft (90–150cm) S 12–16in (30–40cm)	A clump or two of these cheerful daisy-flowered perennials, in warm shades of yellow, or brown, will brighten any border late in the season. As with coneflowers, each bloom has a prominent raised center.
DAYLILIES *Hemerocallis* Z 3–10	H 2–3ft (60–90cm) S 12–18in (30–45cm)	Many selections of these perennials continue to bloom into late summer. The flamboyant, trumpet-shaped flowers come in dazzling hues and exotic combinations of pink, orange, purple, yellow, and red.
NERINES *Nerine bowdenii* Z 8–10	H 18in (45cm) S 12in (30cm)	The elegant, fragile, spidery-looking flowers of these perennials bloom in loose heads. The pink, orange, or white delicate, scented flowers look exotic, but nerines are remarkably sturdy.
KAFFIR LILIES *Schizostylis coccinea* Z 7–9	H 2ft (60cm) S 10–12in (25–30cm)	These perennials produce showy, star-shaped flowers on loose spires from late summer until midautumn. Flowers come in bright red, pink, or white, and the leaves are bright green and sword-shaped.
SHOWY STONECROPS *Sedum spectabile* Z 4–9	H 16–18in (40–45cm) S 16–18in (40–45cm)	In late summer, tiny, starry, usually pink flowers are grouped into dense, often flattened flowerheads on these popular perennials. The leaves are succulent and grayish blue colour.

SITE	CULTIVATION	HINTS AND TIPS
Prefer a moist yet well-drained soil, in part shade or full sun.	Best planted in spring or early summer. Add organic matter before planting, and mulch before the hottest weather to keep the roots cool and moist.	• For best flowering, grow in part shade. • In the first season after planting or in extremely cold areas, protect the crowns over winter. • Divide in spring or take cuttings from sturdy roots in summer (see p.41).
Select a sunny position with well-drained, fertile soil.	Plant in spring, once any late frosts are over. If the soil is poor, incorporate well-rotted compost on planting. Provide support for tall varieties.	• When all flowers and leaves have faded, cut the stems back to 4–6in (10–15cm) above soil level and cover the crowns with a mulch 4in (10cm) deep. In cold or wet areas, cut back, lift the entire plant, and store in a cool greenhouse.
Choose a partly shaded, sheltered spot with well-drained soil.	Plant corms in groups, about 4in (10cm) deep. Incorporate some fertilizer if the soil is poor. Keep them well watered in periods of dry weather.	• Don't let the soil dry out while in leaf, or flowering will be reduced. • The leaves can become quite large, so avoid planting colchicums where they can smother smaller plants in spring.
Fertile, well-drained, moist soil in either full sun or part shade.	Plant corms in groups in late winter or early spring, about 4–6in (10–15cm) apart. Propagate by dividing established clumps every few years in spring.	• Cut back faded flower spikes promptly to encourage good flowering the following year. • Keep well watered in dry weather. • Severe winters can damage them, so mulch with a deep layer of straw, leaves, or similar material.
Choose a sunny spot with any reasonably well-drained soil.	Best planted in spring and autumn. Propagate by dividing established plants in spring or autumn, or take root cuttings (see p.41) in early spring.	• Plant taller types at the back of the border, and provide support if necessary. • Pick the variety 'Robert Bloom' for deep purple-red flowers, or 'White Swan' for white blooms with a hint of green.
Best in a sunny spot with reasonably moist soil.	Plant in autumn or early spring. Incorporate organic matter to encourage the soil to hold moisture. Divide established clumps in autumn or spring.	• If you deadhead after the first flush of flowers fade, a later flush may develop. • Taller heleniums will need some support. • Group several plants of the same variety for a really rich, colorful display.
Reasonably moist soil, in sun to part shade.	Best planted in spring or autumn. Daylilies are easy to grow, although they may take a year to reach their full potential. Consider mulching in dry sites.	• Clumps lose vigor after about four years, so divide them and replant the more vigorous sections in late summer or early spring. • Choose herbaceous daylilies in colder climates; the evergreen types are tender.
Well-drained soil, in full sun, ideally close to a warm wall.	Best planted in spring. In colder areas, protect over winter with a deep layer of loose mulch, or plant in containers that can be sheltered.	• Nerines dislike being disturbed, so leave them alone as long as possible. Divide very congested clumps in late summer so that they have time to reestablish before winter. • Nerines make excellent cut flowers.
Moist but not soggy soil, in sun or part shade.	Best planted in autumn or spring. Keep the soil moist at all times or flowering will be badly affected. Every fourth year, divide congested clumps in spring.	• Where marginally hardy, mulch the crowns with a deep layer of straw, leaves, pine needles, or similar material. • Exciting varieties are 'Major' (crimson), 'Maiden's Blush' (pink) and 'Viscountess Byng' (bright red).
Choose a sunny spot; the soil must not be too heavy or too wet.	Ideally, plant in autumn or spring. Leave the dead flowerheads at the end of the season – they help protect the crowns over winter.	• Other early- and midautumn-flowering sedums well worth growing are 'Ruby Glow' (reddish purple flowers), 'Autumn Joy' (pink, reddening with age), which will grow in a shady spot, and 'Bertram Anderson' (red).

LATE LUXURIANCE
Packed to the gills with color, heleniums are joined by goldenrods, yarrows, bee balms, and roses – proof that the end of summer can still mean bright borders!

HIGH IMPACT *below*
Japanese anemones such as this *Anemone hupehensis* 'September Charm' bring color and height to a late summer or or autumn planting.

Flowers with excellent foliage

WITH MANY FLOWERING plants the blooms hog the limelight, but with these, superb foliage competes with the flowers for top billing in your garden, with the added bonus that it lasts longer. When not in flower, their leaves will provide a foil for other plants in bloom.

OTHER FLOWERS WITH EXCELLENT FOLIAGE

Columbines (*Aquilegia*) pp.94–95	Euphorbias (*Euphorbia*) pp.52–53
Corydalis (*Corydalis*) pp.144–145	Geraniums (*Geranium*) pp.120–121
Cyclamens (*Cyclamen coum*) pp.154–155	Yuccas (*Yucca filamentosa*) pp.140–141

TEXTURE AND TONE, *right*
I'm fascinated by the metallic sheen to the leaves of *Heuchera* 'Pewter Moon'. Their under-surfaces are just as striking, in a bold, rich pink.

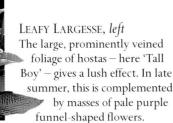

LEAFY LARGESSE, *left*
The large, prominently veined foliage of hostas – here 'Tall Boy' – gives a lush effect. In late summer, this is complemented by masses of pale purple funnel-shaped flowers.

PLANT	SIZE	APPEARANCE
BUGLES *Ajuga reptans* Z 3–9	H 4–10in (10–25cm) S 18in (45cm)	In no time at all, bugles form a dense m of evergreen foliage with (depending on variety) purple, reddish, or variegated le Dense, bright blue or purple flower spi bloom in spring and into early summer
LADY'S MANTLE *Alchemilla mollis* Z 4–7	H 20–24in (50–60cm) S 30–32in (75–80cm)	The rounded, lobed, serrated leaves are slightly downy and grayish green benea lime green flowerheads. Forming a love mound of erect stems, this perennial lo pretty sparkling with raindrops or dew.
CORAL FLOWERS *Heuchera* Z 3–8	H 10–18in (25–45cm) S 8–12in (20–30cm)	The tiny flowers on tall stems that dev in early summer are held above a clump beautifully colored or patterned leaves These perennials often retain most of th foliage for much of the year.
HOSTAS *Hosta* Z 3–8	H 12–24in (30–60cm) S 18–36in (45–90cm)	Magnificent foliage – mainly broad, rounded leaves in lime green, blue-gree silvery blue, often with yellow, cream, white variegation – earns these perenn a place in almost any garden.
DEADNETTLES *Lamium maculatum* Z 4–8	H 8–12in (20–30cm) S 12–24in (30–60cm)	The attractive silver- or white-splashed leaves on these perennials usually look good all year round. They make a good groundcover. Pretty flower spikes in w pink, or red-purple appear in summer.
LUNGWORTS *Pulmonaria* Z 5–8	H 10–12in (25–30cm) S 18–24in (45–60cm)	Although these perennials produce pr purple, red, pink, white, or blue flower in spring, their foliage provides interest all season, with white or silver patterni on dark green.
LONDON PRIDE *Saxifraga × urbium* Z 6–7	H 8–10in (20–25cm) S 2ft (60cm)	This perennial holds its tiny star-shape flowers above unusual rosettes of brigh green foliage. The flowers, held in loos heads, appear in early summer and are white with pink markings.
HENS AND CHICKS *Sempervivum* Z 4–9	H 2–3in (5–7.5cm) S 10–14in (25–35cm)	These evergreen succulents form sprea textural rosettes made up of numerous fleshy, pointed leaves packed tightly together in green and red. Pink flowers tall, fleshy stems appear in summer.
PIGGYBACK PLANT *Tolmiea menziesii* Z 6–9	H 2ft (60cm) S 12in (30cm)	The common name refers to the fact t young plants are formed on mature lea piggyback style. A semievergreen peren it forms a mat of rounded, slightly cri edged, pale green foliage.
VARIEGATED PERIWINKLE *Vinca major* 'Variegata' Z 6–10	H 12in (30cm) S 3ft (90cm)	The arching, spreading stems on this perennial bear pale green leaves with p yellow margins. Throughout mid- and spring they are studded with extremel pretty purple-blue flowers.

SITE	CULTIVATION	HINTS AND TIPS
Any average to moist soil, in sun or shade.	Best planted in spring or autumn. Create new plants by separating off the tiny plants that form on self-rooted stems, or divide in spring or autumn.	• Clipping off early flower spikes when faded may encourage plants to flower into autumn. • I particularly like 'Braunherz' (shiny, dark purple-brown leaves) and 'Burgundy Glow' (with white or pink-red variegation on green).
Very easy to please. Grows in sun or shade and in all but very wet soils.	Ideally, plant in autumn or spring. Propagate by moving tiny plants that have self-seeded to the desired position, or divide clumps in spring or autumn.	• Lady's mantle is easy to grow and readily self-seeds, sometimes to the point of nuisance! • Useful as a gap-filler in almost every conceivable place. Try planting (or letting them self-seed) in the spaces between large paving slabs.
Any moist soil, in sun or part shade.	Best planted in autumn or spring. An annual mulch with leafmold or well-rotted compost keeps growth looking healthy and lush.	• Plants can be divided every couple of years in early autumn. • One of my favorites is 'Pewter Moon', which has purple leaves with distinctive silvery gray marbling on the upper surface.
Most moisture-retentive soils are suitable, in sun, shade, or dappled shade.	Autumn or spring are the best times to plant. An annual mulch of leafmold or compost helps the soil retain moisture.	• Established clumps can be divided in late summer or early spring. • Slugs and snails are a problem, so be prepared to do battle with these pests. Hostas planted in pots fare better, but keep them well watered.
Well-drained soil, in anything but deep shade.	Best planted in autumn or spring. Trim after flowering to keep their dense shape. If they become invasive, divide in autumn or spring.	• Deadnettles bring dry, shaded areas beneath trees and larger shrubs to life. • Pretty varieties are 'Beacon Silver' (pure silver leaves), 'White Nancy' (silver with green edges), and 'Pink Pewter' (pale green with a silvery sheen).
They thrive in reasonably moist soil, in dappled or full shade.	Ideally, plant in autumn or spring. To keep the plants in top condition, water during dry spells and remove faded flowers. Divide mature plants in autumn.	• In mild climates, lungworts may retain their foliage all year. Pick off any deteriorating leaves, which may attract fungal infections. • For leaves that are silver all over, look out for varieties such as *P. saccharata* 'Argentea'.
Needs moist or damp soil with partial shade.	Best planted in autumn or spring. If the soil is not sufficiently moist, add coarse organic matter to aid moisture retention.	• Obtain new plants by separating off individual rosettes with roots from mature plants in autumn or spring. This is also a good way of neatening specimens that have begun to look moth-eaten; replant only the vigorous parts of each plant.
Choose a sunny spot with well-drained, light soil.	Late spring or early summer are the best times to plant. Add plenty of sand if your soil is not very free-draining. Separate off rosettes with roots as new plants.	• Their succulent leaves enable hens and chicks to withstand drought better than most plants grown for lush foliage. • Once a rosette has flowered it dies, but will be replaced by new ones growing around the parent.
Moist, preferably acidic soil, in full or dappled shade.	Best planted in autumn or early spring. Keep plants well watered if the soil gets the slightest bit dry. A mulch helps preserve moisture in the soil.	• Increase stocks by removing and potting up the tiny plants that are produced on the leaves. • For really gorgeous cream- and yellow-blotched leaves, choose 'Variegata' or 'Taff's Gold'. • A useful plant for a groundcover.
Well-drained soil, in part shade or sun.	Ideally, plant in autumn or spring. Propagate by removing rooted stems in autumn or spring. Alternatively, divide established clumps in spring.	• Will grow in quite dense shade, but it may lose some of its variegation and flower less profusely. • An annual mulch after thorough watering helps the plant thrive on soils that tend to get dry. • If it starts to spread too much, cut back in spring.

VERDANT VELVET
The finely toothed, slightly furry leaves of *Alchemilla mollis* look as if they have been cut from a gorgeous, pale green velvet.

LONGTIME COMPANIONS
I've grown lungworts in every garden I've had. Here, *Pulmonaria saccharata* 'Frühlingshimmel' shows off its silvery foliage and blue flowers.

RAINBOW AT YOUR FEET
The crinkly, creeping foliage of bugles makes a good groundcover; for the most striking leaf patterns, choose *Ajuga reptans* 'Multicolor'.

Flowers for groundcover

PLANTS FOR GROUNDCOVER are too often associated in people's minds with the boring, low-maintenance greenery used in some public parks. Not so! All the plants I have chosen here will create a carpet that scores points for both foliage and flowers, as well as helping to suppress weeds.

OTHER FLOWERS FOR GROUNDCOVER

Bugles (*Ajuga reptans*) pp.158–159	Geraniums (*Geranium*) pp.120–121
Elephant's ears (*Bergenia*) pp.144–1445	Deadnettles (*Lamium maculatum*) pp.158–159
Campanulas (*Campanula*) pp.96–97	Periwinkle (*Vinca major*) pp.158–159

CLOUD NINE, *right*
The handsome form of *Tiarella cordifolia* means that plants look equally good grown singly as when used as a groundcover.

VINTAGE BLUE, *left and below*
Like little blue pyramids, the flowerheads of *Muscari armeniacum* — commonly known as grape hyacinth — do look very much like upside-down bunches of grapes.

PLANT	SIZE	APPEARANCE
ROCK CRESS *Arabis* Z 4–8	H 8–10in (20–25cm) S 20–24in (50–60cm)	Forms a dense, gray-green carpet of foli covered in small white or pink flowers from midspring to early summer. The flowers of these often evergreen perenn are held in spikes that get taller as they
AUBRETIA *Aubrieta × cultorum* Z 5–7	H 6–8in (15–20cm) S 2ft (60cm)	Although small, the flowers are so plen and their colors so rich that they make huge impact in spring, especially plante groups. The foliage of this often evergr perennial is covered in very short hairs.
MOUNTAIN AVENS *Dryas × suendermanni* Z 3–6	H 8in (20cm) S 2ft (60cm)	This perennial creates an evergreen carp of tiny leaves similar in shape to oak lea From late spring until midsummer, gorgeous nodding white flowers with bright yellow stamens appear.
ENGLISH BLUEBELLS *Hyacinthoides non-scripta* Z 4–9	H 10–12in (25–30cm) S 6in (15cm)	Could there be a more glorious sight in l spring than trees standing in a sea of Eng bluebells? The flower spikes of these bul are draped with miniature hanging bell white, rich blue, or pale pink.
GRAPE HYACINTHS *Muscari* Z 3–8	H 4–8in (10–20cm) S 4–6in (10–15cm)	In spring these bulbs produce dense, al conical spikes of tiny blue or white flow with a slight fragrance. The leaves are grayish green and narrow. Try growing under shrubs in miniature drifts.
KNOTWEED *Persicaria bistorta* 'Superba' Z 4–8	H 3ft (90cm) S 2ft (60cm)	Shaped like prettily colored bottle brus dense, bright pink flower spikes are produced above mounds of light green foliage from late spring to midsummer. A perennial, it is semievergreen.
FRINGE CUPS *Tellima grandiflora* Z 4–8	H 32in (80cm) S 2ft (60cm)	This herbaceous perennial thrives in co shaded situations. Its foliage is light gre rounded, and lobed, and flower spikes of tiny, yellowish green bells appear from spring until early summer.
FOAM FLOWER *Tiarella cordifolia* Z 3–7	H 6in (15cm) S 18in (45cm)	Like waves of white froth, loose flower spikes of tiny, star-shaped, creamy whit flowers waft above the pale green, lobec foliage in spring. This perennial forms a attractive evergreen carpet.
NASTURTIUMS *Tropaeolum majus* Annual	H 8–10in (20–30cm) S 8–10in (20–30cm)	These annuals produce a fiery display o large, open flowers throughout the summer. The bluish green leaves are ne circular. Varieties are available in cream yellow, orange, and reddish orange.
LESSER PERIWINKLE *Vinca minor* Z 4–9	H 8in (20cm) S 30in (75cm)	This evergreen perennial is grown for it long, trailing stems that break out in p pink, white, or bluish purple flowers fr spring until early summer. Variegated forms are available.

SITE	CULTIVATION	HINTS AND TIPS
Well-drained soil, in plenty of sun.	Best planted in spring. Once most of the flowers have faded, trim the plant with shears to keep it bushy. Plants can be divided as soon as flowering is over.	• Rock cress will grow in both a fairly heavy soil and in shade, but the foliage will be less dense and flowering less prolific. • For interesting variegated foliage with distinct, pale yellow leaf margins, try 'Variegata'.
Well-drained, preferably alkaline soil and plenty of sun.	Ideally, plant in spring. They will grow better in slightly acidic soils that have been limed first. Divide plants in late summer.	• Once flowering is over, you can give plants a "haircut" with shears to keep them compact. • If the plants start to look patchy, divide in late summer and replant vigorous sections only. • Ideal for planting in gaps in stone walls.
Needs free-draining, preferably acid soil and plenty of sun.	Spring is the best time for planting. Add extra sand and acidic material such as oak leafmold to improve the drainage and acidity of the soil if needed.	• Take semiripe cuttings in summer. • Leave the faded flowers on the plants to allow the attractive, silky seedheads to develop. • This is a small-scale groundcover plant for use with other small plants – try it among alpines.
A moist but not soggy spot, in dappled shade.	Best planted about 5–6in (13–15cm) deep, as soon as the bulbs are available in late summer. Self-seeds readily but takes 5 years to grow into flowering bulbs.	• Allow bulbs to naturalize and form drifts beneath groups of trees. Choose the smaller-flowered forms for a more natural effect. • Bluebells can multiply to the point where they become a nuisance, so beware of them in borders.
Choose a sunny spot with reasonably well-drained soil.	Plant the bulbs 2–3in (5–7.5cm) deep in late summer or autumn. They are very easy to please and need little care. Divide established clumps every few years.	• Unusual edging for paths or borders, but they are invasive and may outgrow their welcome. • They look great in containers and windowboxes. • They will grow fairly well in part shade but will flower less profusely.
Thrives in moist but well-drained soil, in sun or part shade.	Best planted in autumn or spring. Regular watering is advisable, at least until it establishes; subsequent growth will be much more rapid.	• Divide established clumps in autumn or spring. • Will do quite well in shade, where flowers and foliage both tend to be rather paler in color. • The flowers of knotweed make unusual cut flowers that last well.
Well-drained but moist soil, in a cool spot in dappled shade.	Ideally, plant in autumn or spring. Divide established clumps in autumn or spring to rejuvenate them.	• Water regularly if there is any danger of the soil drying out; this is particularly important when the plants are establishing. • In severe winters or very cold gardens, protect for winter with loose straw, leaves, or pine needles.
Cool, moisture-retentive, ideally acidic soil, in partial shade.	Best planted in autumn or spring, incorporating leafmold to improve soil texture if necessary. Divide established plants in autumn or spring.	• Planted beneath trees and shrubs, foam flowers make a particularly pretty groundcover. • This foam flower has a creeping habit and will gradually develop a spread of close to 2ft (60cm). • In winter the foliage turns an attractive brown.
Well-drained soil, in full sun.	They dislike too dry a soil, so add organic matter if the soil is light. Sow seed indoors in spring. Harden off, then plant out after the late frosts.	• Plant them 8–10in (20–25cm) apart to make a good groundcover on a sunny site. • Nasturtiums also make great container plants. Water regularly so that they don't get dry, and don't overfeed them or they will not flower.
Any reasonably well-drained soil, in full sun or part shade.	Best planted in autumn or spring. If the soil tends to dry out, add coarse organic matter at planting. Mulching will also help strong growth as plants establish.	• It grows quickly, and if planted at 2ft (60cm) intervals will soon form a good groundcover. • To increase your plant stocks, sever and replant those stems that have formed their own root systems.

VARIATIONS ON A THEME
Most nasturtiums have plain green foliage, but for interest even when not flower try this variegated form, *Tropaeolum majus* 'Alaska'.

REFORMED CHARACTER
The mere mention of knotweed fills most gardeners with fear, but this cultivated form, *Periscaria bistorta* 'Superba', looks good and is easy to control.

CHARM SCHOOL
Like other rock cresses, this rich pink *Arabis blepharophylla* 'Spring Charm' is equally useful growing in rock gardens and borders. I also love to see it planted in gaps in a stone wall.

Glossary

Words in *italics* within a definition have a separate entry.

ANNUAL A plant that completes its life cycle (growing from seed, flowering, setting seed, and dying) within one year.

BACKFILL Replace soil or soil mix around roots after planting.

BEDDING PLANT Plants (usually *annuals*, but sometimes *biennials* and *perennials*) that are used for temporary, often showy, display.

BIENNIAL A plant that produces leafy growth in the first year and then flowers, sets seed, and dies the next.

BRACT A modified leaf at the base of a flower or flower cluster. Bracts may resemble normal leaves or be reduced and scalelike in appearance; they are often large and brightly colored.

BULB A group of swollen, modified, underground leaves that acts as a storage organ.

COMPOST An organic material resulting from the rotting down of organic material from the kitchen and garden.

CORM An underground, bulblike, swollen stem or stem base.

CROWN The part of a *herbaceous plant* where the stems meet the roots and from where new shoots develop.

CUTTING A piece of stem, root, or leaf that, if taken at the correct time of year and prepared and cared for in the correct way, will grow to form a new plant. Basal stem cutting: one taken from the base of a (usually *herbaceous*) plant as it begins to produce growth in spring. Root cutting: one taken from part of a semimature or mature root. Semiripe cutting: one taken from half-ripened wood during the growing season. Softwood cutting: one taken from young, immature growth during the growing season.

DEADHEADING The removal of spent flowers or flowerheads to promote further growth or flowering, prevent seeding, or improve appearance.

DIVISION The lifting and dividing of a plant clump into small pieces, which are then replanted.

DWARF Naturally small-growing mutation of a plant, often vegetatively propagated to produce a named dwarf variety.

f. (*forma*, form) Applied to plants within a species that differ in some minor character.

GENUS A group of related species linked by common characters, e.g. *Digitalis* (foxgloves).

HERBACEOUS PLANT One with top-growth that is soft, not woody, and (usually) dies back over winter.

HYBRID The offspring of genetically different parents, usually of distinct *species*.

LEAFMOLD Fibrous, flaky material derived from decomposed leaves, used as an ingredient in potting mixes and as a soil amendment.

MULCH A material applied in a layer to the soil surface to suppress weeds, conserve moisture, and maintain a relatively uniform root temperature. In addition to organic materials such as manure, bark, and compost, plastic, paper, and gravel may also be used.

NAMED VARIETY See *variety*.

PERENNIAL A plant, usually *herbaceous*, that lives for at least three years.

POTTING ON Transferring a plant from a small pot to a larger one.

POTTING UP Transferring seedlings into individual pots of soil mix.

PROPAGATING CASE A covered tray that provides a humid atmosphere for seedlings or other plants being propagated. Some have an electrical heating element in the base.

RHIZOME A swollen stem that grows horizontally, producing roots and shoots.

SEED A ripened, fertilized ovule containing a dormant embryo capable of developing into an adult plant.

SOIL MIX A prepared growing medium available in different formulas, for example multipurpose, cuttings, and seed soil mix.

SPECIES A category in plant classification within a *genus*, denoting closely related similar plants.

SUBSP. (subspecies) A subdivision of a species, higher in rank than *varietas* or *forma*.

TUBER A thickened, usually underground, storage organ.

VAR. (*varietas*, variety) Naturally occurring variant of a wild species, exhibiting a characteristic (often in flower color) that is different from the typical *species* and can be maintained through propagation.

VARIETY A cultivated variety of a plant as distinct from a wild, naturally occurring variant, also known as a "cultivar."

VARIEGATED Marked with one or more colors. Often used to describe leaves with white, yellow, or cream markings.

✕ Sign denoting a *hybrid*.

Index

Where there are several references, the main entries are indicated in **bold**.
References in *italics* refer to illustrations. Where the common and Latin plant names
are the same, only the Latin name is used.

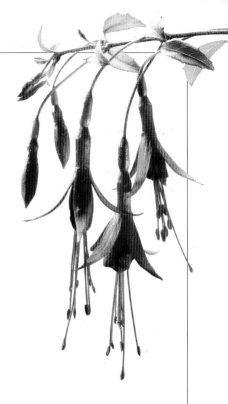

Acknowledgments

AUTHOR'S ACKNOWLEDGMENTS
My thanks to Jenny Jones, Jane Bull, Annabel Morgan, Louise Abbott, Lee Griffiths, David Lamb, Anne-Marie Bulat and everyone else at Dorling Kindersley for their help and enthusiasm in putting this book together, to Dave King for his fantastic photographs, and to Alasdair, who carried on with everything, including the digging, once "the bump" had got too big.

PUBLISHER'S ACKNOWLEDGMENTS
Editorial assistance Diana Vowles, Tanis Smith. Additional DTP design Sonia Charbonnier. Overseas liaison Alison Rich. Index Ella Skene.

WE EXTEND SPECIAL THANKS TO THE FOLLOWING FOR THEIR HELP:
Forest Lodge Garden Centre
Holt Pound, Farnham, Surrey GU10 4LD
Hopleys Plants Ltd
Much Hadham, Herts SG10 6BU
Kelways Ltd
Langport, Somerset TA10 9EZ

PICTURE CREDITS
The publisher would like to thank the following for their kind permission to reproduce their photographs:

a=above; c=center; b=below; l=left; r=right; t=top
A-Z BOTANICAL LTD: D W Bevan 26cr. HEATHER ANGEL: 36cl. BRUCE COLEMAN COLLECTION: Kim Taylor 10tl. MELANIE ECLARE: 41c, 48–49, 60br, 61c. THE GARDEN PICTURE LIBRARY: Brian Carter 86br; Kathy Charlton 141cr; Ron Evans 128–129; John Ferro Sims 11bc, 67cr; John Glover 12c, 84cl, 120br, 126tl, 127tr; Juliet Greene 82c; Marijke Heuff 103tr; Michael Howes 112br; Jacqui Hurst 57c, 69bl; Lamontagne 11br; Mayer/Le Scanff 2, 85bl, 102c, 103tl; Jerry Pavia 63tl; Howard Rice 11c, 13tc, 30-31, 42b, 114cr; J S Sira 94br; Juliette Wade 46tr, 99tl; Didier Willery 111br, 118crb; Steven Wooster 47br, 64–65, 71tc, 129tr, 157tr. JOHN GLOVER PHOTOGRAPHY: 26br, 34bc, 63tr, 72br, 74cr, 90–91, 93br, 97br, 113c, 120. JERRY HARPUR: 33tl, 39tc, 40l, 54cl, 55br, 76–77, 78bl, 88br, 97tr, 104br, 119bl, 125tr, 129 (garden designed by Simon Hopkinson). SANDRA HYTCH: 5tr, 58c, 122–123. ANDREW LAWSON: 6–7, 12cl, 12–13, 13tr, 35, 40cl, 45cl, 53, 54cr, 59bl, 66c, 68cl, 81tr, 92cl (Brook Cottage, Alkerton), 94cl, 94cr, 97c, 109tr, 111tr, 115bl, 124bl, 126clb, bc, 126–127, 127br, 128tl, bl, c, 132cl, 154 cl. CLIVE NICHOLS: 37tc (Sticky Wicket, Dorset), 38r, 50bl (Bassibones Farm, Bucks.), 57tl (Vale End, Surrey), 68tr, 73c, 101cl (Greystone Cottage, Oxon.), 112tr, 118cl, c, cr, 134 cl, 135 tr, 144cl (Greystone Cottage, Oxon.). PHOTOS HORTICULTURAL: 27bl. PICTOR INTERNATIONAL: 129tc. HOWARD RICE: 79bl, 95. TIM SANDALL: 27c & r. JULIETTE WADE: 72cr.

JACKET: MELANIE ECLARE: back tcl; front bc; inside front bc. THE GARDEN PICTURE LIBRARY: Howard Rice back tr. JOHN GLOVER: back bl, front bl, tr. JERRY HARPUR: back tl, front tcl. ANDREW LAWSON: back br; inside front br; spine t. CLIVE NICHOLS: front tl, br.

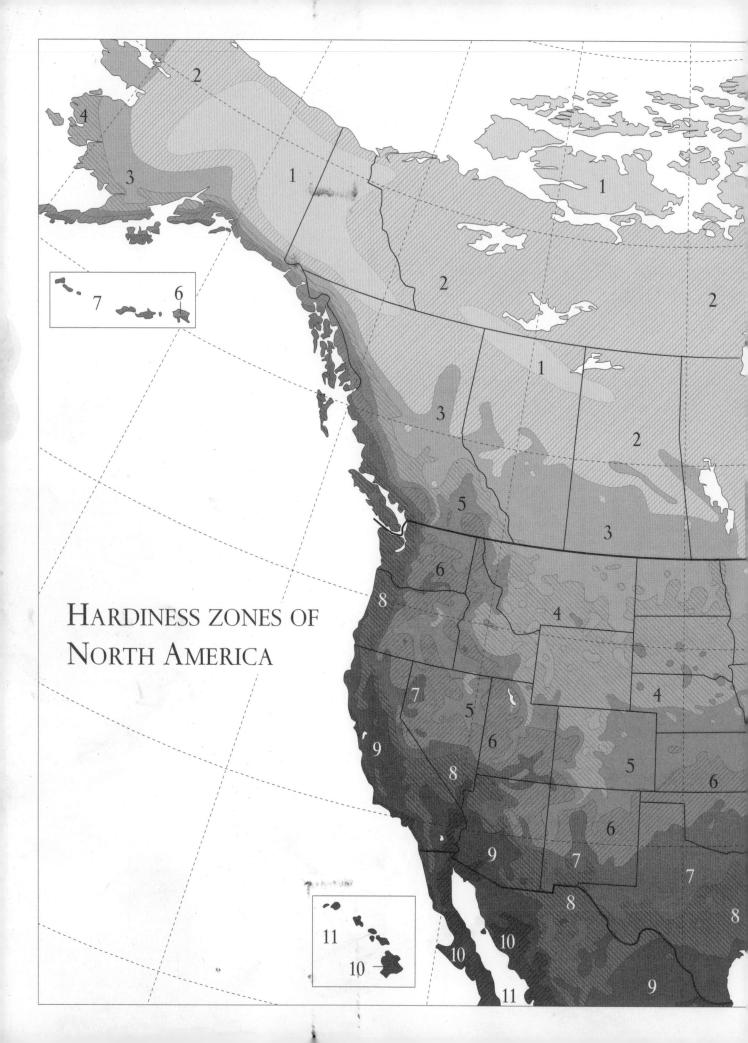

HARDINESS ZONES OF
NORTH AMERICA